NEW Cornerstone

1

STUDENT EDITION
with Digital Resources

New Cornerstone 1

Pearson, 221 River Street, Hoboken, NJ 07030

Cover credit: CS1_U1_SE_Cover Brian Jackson/123RF

Library of Congress Cataloging-in-Publication Data
A catalog record for the print edition is available from the Library of Congress.

The publishers would like to recognize the contributions of our original Series Consultants, Anna Uhl Chamot, Jim Cummins, and Sharroky Hollie. This edition is published in memory of Dr. Chamot, an extraordinary educator, writer, and scholar.

ISBN-10: 0-13-523194-9 (with Digital Resources)
ISBN-13: 978-0-13-523194-4 (with Digital Resources)
1 18

www.english.com/cornerstone

Consultants and Reviewers

Carlos Eduardo Aguilar Cortés
Universidad de La Salle
Bogotá, Colombia

Rebecca Anselmo
Sunrise Acres Elementary School
Las Vegas, NV, USA

Ana Applegate
Redlands School District
Redlands, CA, USA

Terri Armstrong
Houston ISD
Houston, TX, USA

José Augusto Lugo
Cerros
Bogotá, Colombia

Jacqueline Avritt
Riverside County Office of Ed.
Hemet, CA, USA

Mitchell Bobrick
Palm Beach County School
West Palm Beach, FL, USA

Victoria Brioso-Saldala
Broward County Schools
Fort Lauderdale, FL, USA

Brenda Carbarga Schubert
Creekside Elementary School
Salinas, CA, USA

Gabriela Cecilia Díaz
Grilli Canning College
Buenos Aires, Argentina

Joshua Ezekiel
Bardin Elementary School
Salinas, CA, USA

Valeria Goluza
Grilli Canning College
Buenos Aires, Argentina

Veneshia Gonzalez
Seminole Elementary School
Okeechobee, FL, USA

Carolyn Grigsby
San Francisco Unified School District
San Francisco, CA, USA

Julie Grubbe
Plainfield Consolidated Schools
Chicago, IL, USA

Yasmin Hernandez-Manno
Newark Public Schools
Newark, NJ, USA

Do Thi Thanh Hien
The Asian International School
Ho Chi Minh City, Vietnam

Janina Kusielewicz
Clifton Public Schools/Bilingual Ed.
& Basic Skills Instruction Dept.
Clifton, NJ, USA

Mary Helen Lechuga
El Paso ISD
El Paso, TX, USA

Gayle P. Malloy
Randolph School District
Randolph, MA, USA

Le Tue Minh
Wellspring International Bilingual School
Hanoi, Vietnam

Minh Phuong Nguyen
CIEM-Education
Hanoi, Vietnam

Patricia Parroquiano
Gimnasio Campestre Reino Británico
Bogotá, Colombia

Adriano De Paula Souza
Liceu Jardim
Santo André, Brazil

Randy Payne
Patterson/Taft Elementaries
Mesa, AZ, USA

María Eugenia Pérez de Castro
Escuela Primaria Puerta Abierta
Buenos Aires, Argentina

Carolina Pérez Martínez
Thomas Jefferson School
Xalapa, Mexico

Lucy Reyes
Colegio Axis
Mexicali, B.C., Mexico

Sergio Rivera
Liceo Hermano Miguel La Salle
Bogotá, Colombia

Marcie L. Schnegelberger
Alisal Union SD
Salinas, CA, USA

Delphine Sichler
Keystone International Education
Córdoba, Mexico

Lorraine Smith
Collier County Schools
Naples, FL, USA

Shawna Stoltenborg
Glendale Elementary School
Glen Burnie, MD, USA

Kampanart Thammaphati
Wattana Wittaya Academy
Thailand

Hoang Dieu Thu
Edison Schools
Vietnam

Denise Tiffany
West High School
Iowa City, IA, USA

Letter Sounds

a	a-e, ai, ay	b	c, -ck, k	d	e
e-e, e, ee, ea	f	g	h	i	i-e, -y, i, igh
j, ge, -dge	l	m	n	o	o-e, o, oa, oe, ow
p	qu	r	s, ci, ce	t	u
u-e, -ew, ou, -ue, oo	v	w	x	y	z

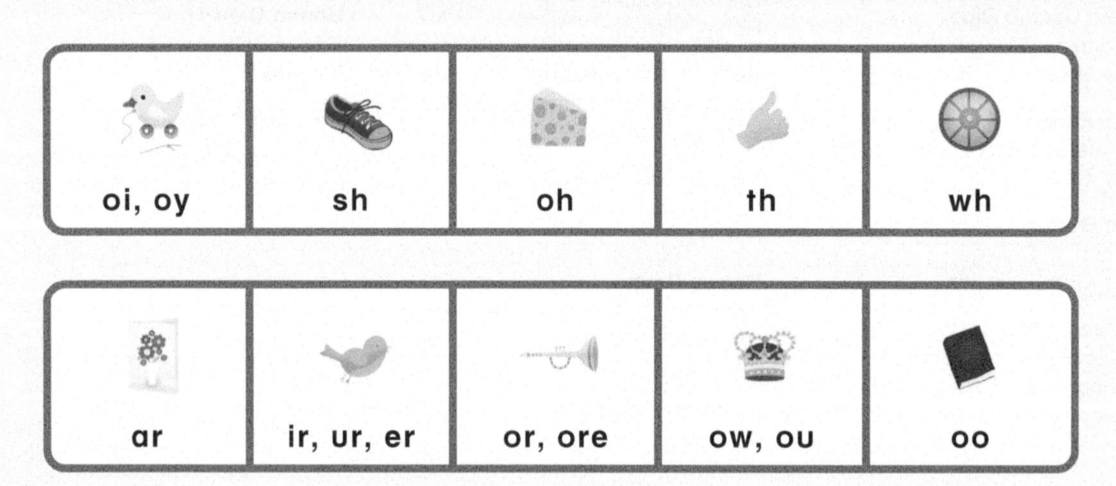

Welcome to ***New Cornerstone***!

We wrote ***New Cornerstone*** to help you learn to read, write, and speak English. We wrote a book that will make learning English and learning to read a lot of fun.

New Cornerstone includes a mix of all subjects. We have written some make-believe stories and some true stories.

As you use this program, you will build on what you already know, learn new words and new information, and take part in projects. The projects will help you improve your English skills.

Learning a language takes time, but just like learning to swim or ride a two-wheeler, it is fun!

We hope you enjoy ***New Cornerstone***, and we wish you success on every step of your learning journey.

Unit 1

Contents

Changes

Reading 3

Put It All Together

Unit 2

Contents

Communities

Unit 3

Contents

Traditions

Unit Preview

Reading 1

Reading 2

Reading 3

Put It All Together

Unit 4

Contents

Animals and Plants

Reading 3

Put It All Together

Unit 5

Contents

One World

Reading 3

Put It All Together

Unit 6

Contents

Friendships

Unit 1 Changes

Sometimes change is hard. But sometimes change is fun! Name some things that change. How do they change? Tell the class.

THE BIG QUESTION
How will you change this year as you meet new friends?
View and Respond
Watch the video. What is it about?
Talk about the poster. What do you see?
Visit Pearson English Portal.

Build Unit Background

What Do You Know about Changes?

Use what you know.

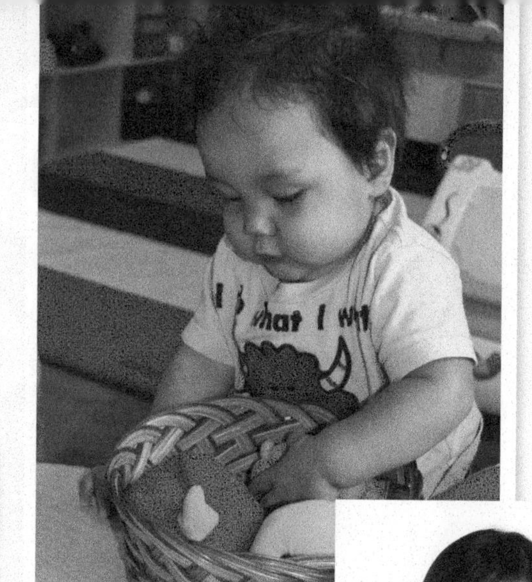

Children grow.

Flowers bloom.

Weather changes.

We make new friends.

Your Turn

Think about a change
in your life.
Tell the class about it.

Build Unit Background

Sing about Changes

Changing Seasons

In fall, we rake the leaves.
In winter, we play in snow.
All throughout the year,
the seasons come and go.

Flowers grow in spring.
The summer breezes blow.
All throughout the year,
the seasons come and go.

Reading Tip

We read English from left to right and top to bottom.

Vocabulary

These words will help you understand the reading.

Words to Know

1. I like my new book.
2. I give my book to you.

3. I have a new backpack.

Sight Words

like
my
you

Story Words

new
backpack

Your Turn

Pick one word from either box.
Use the word in a sentence.
Ask your teacher for help.

3

Phonics

Short *a; d, m, s*

Listen for the sound at the beginning of the word. Say the sound.

Your Turn

Which letter stands for the sound at the beginning of the word?

a d m

d m s

a d m

a m s

Story Preview

Who is in the story?

Sam

mother

Sam

Where does the story happen?

home

school

Reading Strategy | **Preview**

Look at the pictures. What is the story about? As you read, see how previewing helps you understand the story.

Reading 1

I Am Sam

by Pamela Walker
illustrated by Kathryn Mitter

I am Sam.

I like my shoes.

I like my backpack.

I am sad.

I am new.

I am Sam.

I am Sam.

I am happy.

I love you.

Think It Over

Read the questions. Say the answers.
Use Sight Words and Story Words.

1. Who does Sam meet at school?
2. Why is Sam sad?
3. How does Sam feel at the end of the story?
4. How do you make new friends?

Reading Strategy	Preview
How did previewing the story help you understand it?	

5–6

Grammar and Writing

Be Verbs

Use ***I am*** + name or ***I am*** + adjective to talk about you.

I am Ana.
I am happy.

Use ***not*** to talk about things that are not true.

I am not sad.

I am → **I'm**

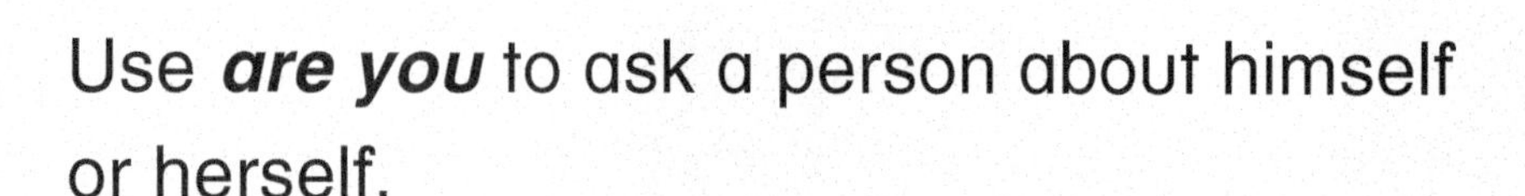

Use ***are you*** to ask a person about himself or herself.

Are you Paco? Yes, **I am.** No, **I'm not. I'm** Julio.

Practice A

Use *am* or *are* to fill in the blanks.

1. I ____am____ happy.
2. You ________ sad.
3. I ________ tired.
4. You ________ not six years old.

Practice B

Write the sentences from Practice A.
Use *I'm* or *You're*.

1. ______________________________.
2. ______________________________.
3. ______________________________.
4. ______________________________.

Apply

Example: A: Are you new?

B: Yes, I am.

Are you six? Are you sad? Are you happy?

Write

Draw a picture of your face. Write about you.

I am Lee. I am new.
I am happy.

7–8

Vocabulary

These words will help you understand the reading.

Sight Words

see

is

little

Story Words

butterfly

frog

Words to Know

1. I see a kitten.
2. The kitten is little.

3. I see a butterfly.

4. Can you see the frog?

Your Turn

Pick one word from either box.

Use the word in a sentence.

9

Phonics

Short *e*; *f*, *l*, *t*

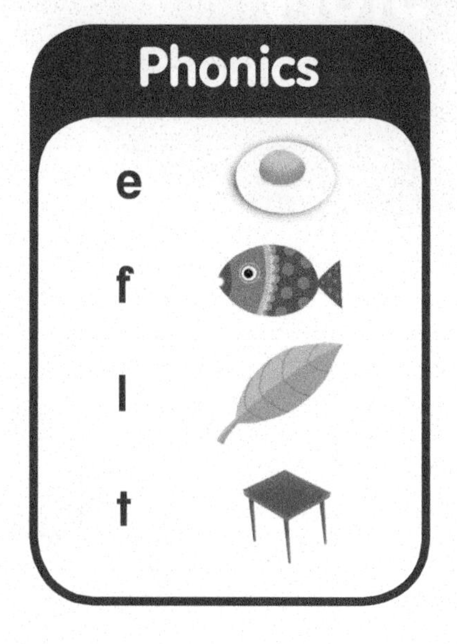

Listen for the sound at the beginning of the word. Say the sound.

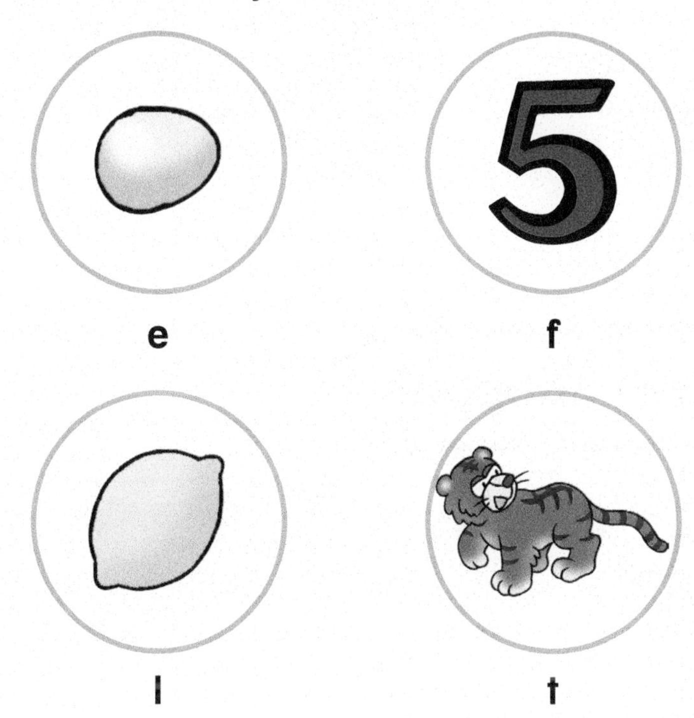

Your Turn

Which letter stands for the sound at the beginning of the word?

f l t e f l e l t e f t

Story Preview

Who is in the story?

caterpillar

frog

Where does the story happen?

tree

pond

Reading Strategy | **Sequence**

Sequence tells when things happen in order. What is the sequence of this story? As you read, see how things happen in order.

I Met Ted

On Your Own

by Christian Foley
illustrated by Don Tate

I am a caterpillar.

I am little.

I met Ted.

Ted is a tadpole.

See Ted.

Ted is a fat tadpole.

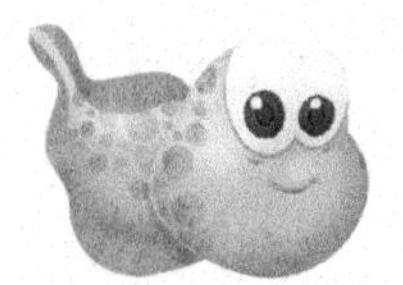

He is a fat, fat tadpole.

Ted is big.
He sits and sits.

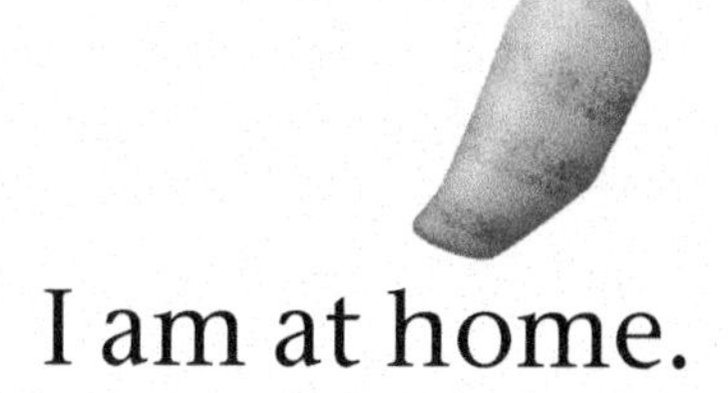

I am at home.

Ted is a frog.
I am a butterfly.

Think It Over

Read the questions. Say the answers.
Use Sight Words and Story Words.

1. What is the tadpole's name?
2. What happened to the butterfly?
3. What happened to Ted?
4. How have you changed since you were a baby?

Speaking Tip

To check if you understood the story, tell it to a classmate.

Reading Strategy | **Sequence**

How did following the sequence in the story help you understand it?

11–12

A CLOSER LOOK AT...

Frogs

A frog begins as an egg.

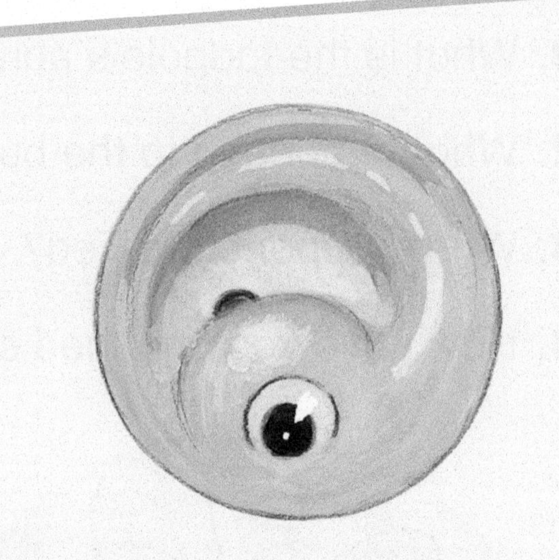

It is now a tadpole.

Back legs grow.

Front legs grow.

It is now a frog.

Activity to Do

Draw pictures to show change.

- Draw a tadpole.
- Draw a frog.
- Talk about your pictures.

Grammar and Writing

Pronouns: *He, She, It*

Use ***he*** for a boy or man, ***she*** for a girl or woman, and ***it*** for a thing. Use the verb ***is*** with ***he***, ***she***, and ***it***.

She is a girl.
He is a boy.
He is not a girl.
It's a backpack.

He is	→	**he's**
She is	→	**she's**
It is	→	**It's**
is not	→	**isn't**

To ask a question, use ***is*** before ***he***, ***she***, or ***it***.

Is he six? No, **he isn't**.

Practice A

Fill in the blank with *he*, *she*, or *it*.

1. She is sitting on a chair.
2. ____________ is jumping.
3. ____________ is on the floor.

Practice B

Fill in the blank with *he's*, *she's*, or *it's*.

1.  He's eating a carrot.
2.  __________ riding a horse.
3. 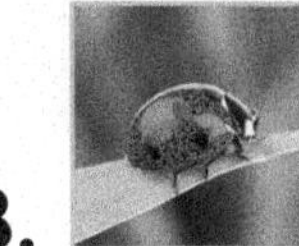 __________ on the plant.

Apply

Example: A: Is he seven?

B: No, he isn't. He's six.

Is she new?
Is he happy?
Is she six?

Write

Draw a picture of a classmate. Write about your classmate.

She is Lucy. She is six.
She is happy.

13–14

Vocabulary

These words will help you understand the reading.

Words to Know

1. Do you have a snack for me?

Sight Words

have
me
too

2. My hat is too big.

Story Words

three
fun

3. Three pals have fun.

Your Turn

Pick one word from either box.

Use the word in a sentence.

15

Phonics

Short *i; n, p*

Listen for the sound at the beginning of the word. Say the sound.

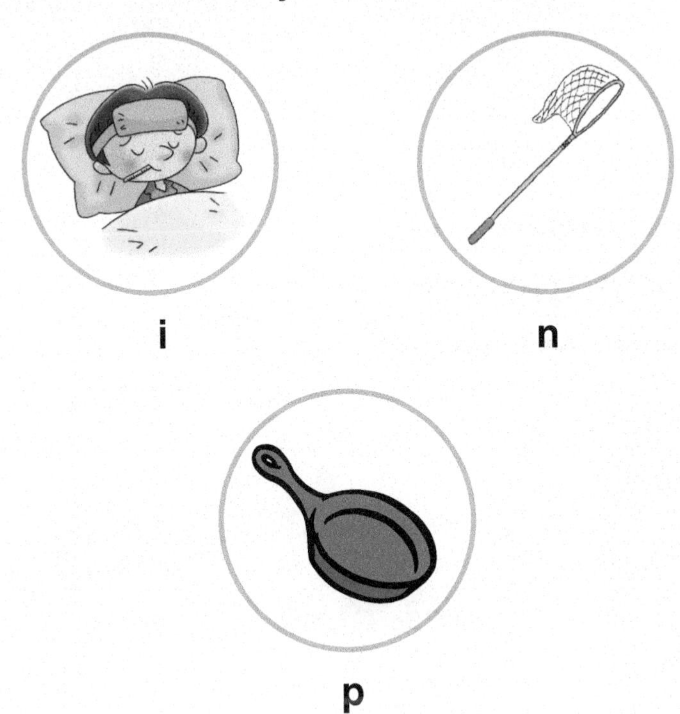

Your Turn

Which letter stands for the sound at the beginning of the word?

i n p

i n p

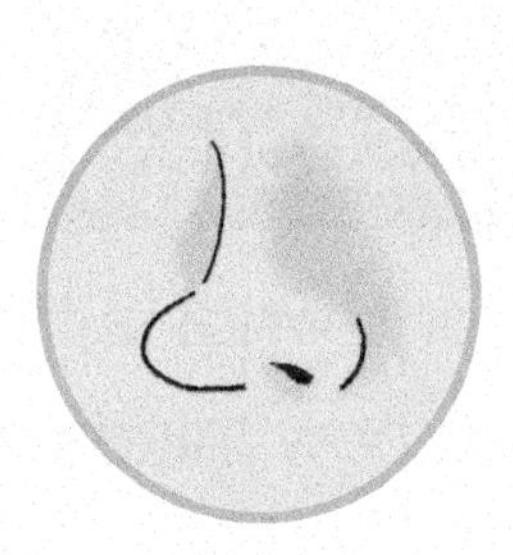

i n p

i n p

Story Preview

Who is in the story?

Tip

Kim

pals

Where does the story happen?

city

country

Reading Strategy Compare and Contrast

In the story, what is the same? What is different? As you read, see how things are alike and different.

Shared Reading Your teacher will show you how to use the strategy. Listen, watch, and practice.

Tip

On Your Own

by Katrinka Moore
illustrated by Mary Roja

I am Kim.
I have a dog.
His name is Tip.
I am sad.
Tip is sad, too.

I can see Tip in the van.
He can see me, too.
Goodbye, Tip.

Tip is at his new home.
He has three new pals.

Ann, Ed, and Mel play with him.

Tip is not too sad.
He has fun in his new home!

Read the questions. Say the answers.
Use Sight Words and Story Words.

1. Who is Kim?
2. Why is Tip sad?
3. What is Tip's new home like?
4. How do you feel in a new place?

Speaking Tip

Practice asking for information. Ask a partner a question about the story. Use Sight and Story Words.

Reading Strategy **Compare and Contrast**

How did comparing and contrasting parts of the story help you understand it?

17–18

Grammar and Writing

Pronouns: *We, They*

Use ***we*** for you and other people. ***They*** is for two or more people, places, or things. Use ***are*** with *we* and *they*.

> **We are** at school. **We are not** at home.

To ask a question, use ***are*** before *we* or *they*.

> **Are they** busy?
> Yes, **they are.**

We are	→	**We're**
They are	→	**They're**
are not	→	**aren't**

Practice A

Fill in the blanks with *we* or *they*.

1. ___We___ are pals.
2. ________ are at school.
3. ________ are not my toys.
4. ________ are my sister's toys.

Practice B

Read the questions in Apply. Change them into sentences. Write the sentences in your notebook.

Example: *Are we in class?*
We are in class.

Apply

Example: A: *Are we in class?*
B: *Yes, we are.*

Are they pals?
Are they students?
Are we teachers?

Write

Draw a picture of your class. Write about your class.

We are in class.
Ms. Lopez is my teacher.
Lee and Jin are students.
They are my pals.

WB 19–20

Put It All Together

Projects

Your teacher will help you choose one of these projects.

Written 

Write about a new friend.

Write a story to tell about a new friend.

THE BIG QUESTION

How will you change this year as you meet new friends? Talk about it.

Oral

Introduce a new friend.

Introduce a new friend to your class.

Visual/Active

Draw a new friend.

Draw pictures to show what your new friend looks like.

21–22

Listening and Speaking Workshop

Describe a Good Friend

Tell the class about a good friend.

1 Prepare

Think about a good friend. Draw a picture of him or her. Write three sentences to describe your friend.

1. Anna is my best friend.
2. She is seven.
3. She has a brother.

2 Practice and Present

Show the picture of your friend to the class. Use the sentences you wrote. Describe your friend to the class.

Useful Language

Listen and repeat.

Who is your best friend? How old is he/she? Does he/she have any brothers or sisters?

As you speak, do this:

- Say each word clearly.
- Say your sentences slowly.
- Use the same sentence type as the examples.

Listening Tip

Listen to your teacher. Learn the expression, *my best friend*. Who is your best friend?

As you listen, do this:

- Look at the picture.
- Listen for words that describe the picture.
- How do the picture and the words help you understand what people say?
- If you don't understand, ask questions.

3 Evaluate

Ask yourself these questions:

- Did you describe your friend well?
- You listened for words. How did that help you understand what people said?

Writing Workshop

Write a Paragraph

You will write a paragraph. A paragraph is a group of sentences about something.

I am Min. I am six. My sister is Lian. She's four. My dad is Deshi. He is fun. My mom is Jia. She is nice. I love my family.

① **Prewrite** List the people in your family in a chart. Tell something about each person.

Carlos listed his ideas in this chart.

Person	Name	Something about him/her
me	Carlos	six
mother	Luz	smart
father	Oscar	brave

2 **Draft** Write a paragraph. Use the ideas in your chart. Use new words from the unit.

3 **Revise** Read your paragraph. Use the Revising Checklist to make your writing better.

Revising Checklist

- ✔ Did I tell about each person?
- ✔ Are all the sentences about my family?

Here is Carlos's paragraph.

I am Carlos. I am six. My mother is Luz. She's smart. My father is Oscar. He's brave. We are a happy family.

Spelling Tip

Say a word aloud to help you spell it.

4. **Edit** Trade papers. Correct your partner's paragraph. Use the Checklist.

5. **Publish** Make a clean copy of your paragraph. Share it with the class.

Editing Checklist

- ✔ Each sentence starts with a capital letter.
- ✔ Each sentence ends with a period.
- ✔ Contractions are correct (*he's, isn't*).

WB
23–24

Fluency

For Each Reading...

1. Listen to the sentences.
2. Listen and use your finger to follow the words.
3. Listen, use your finger, and say the words.

Sam has a new school.

I Am Sam

Ted is a fat tadpole.

I Met Ted

Tip has three new pals.

Tip

WB 25–26

Unit 2

Communities

Some communities are big. Some communities are small. We all live in a community.

THE BIG QUESTION

Who are the people who help in your community?

View and Respond

Watch the video. What is it about?

Talk about the poster. What do you see?

Visit Pearson English Portal.

Build Unit Background

What Do You Know about Communities?

Use what you know.

A city is a community.

A small town is a community.

A teacher works in a community.

People live and work in a community.

Your Turn

Think about a place in your community.

Tell the class about it.

Build Unit Background

Sing about Communities

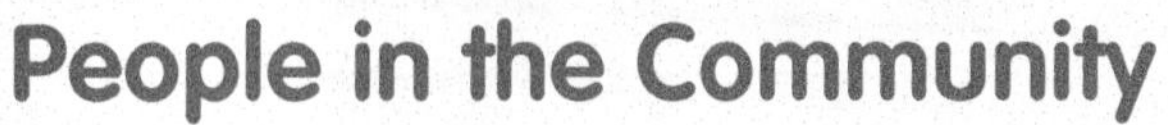

People in the Community

The people on the street say,
"Hello, hello, hello."
"Hello, hello, hello."
"Hello, hello, hello."
The people on the street say,
"Hello, hello, hello,"
all over town.

The driver on the bus says,

"Hello, hello, hello."

"Hello, hello, hello."

"Hello, hello, hello."

The driver on the bus says,

"Hello, hello, hello,"

all over town.

Reading Tip

We read English from left to right and top to bottom.

Reading 1
Prepare to Read

These words will help you understand the reading.

Sight Words

he

she

about

Story Words

people

letter

Vocabulary

Words to Know

1. Rosa asks for help.

2. He can help.

3. She asks about his important job.

4. People can mail a letter.

Your Turn

Pick a word from either box.

Use the word in a sentence.

29

Phonics

Short *o*; *c*, *h*

Look at each picture and word.

Listen to the letter sounds.

Say the word.

Phonics	
o	
c	
h	

hot

doll

on

cat

Your Turn

Sound out the words. Point to the word for the picture.

dog dig

hit fit

pot pat

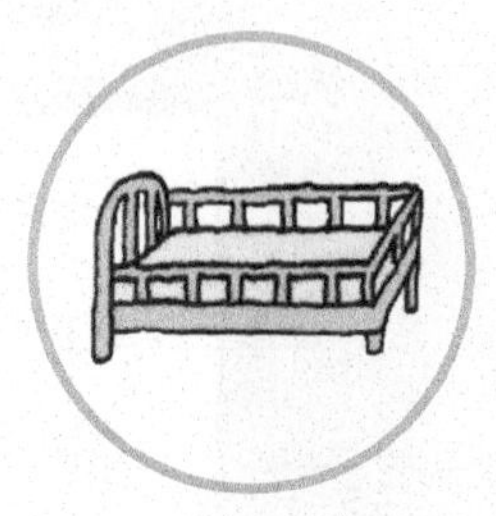

hot cot

Story Preview

bus driver

Who is in this story?

veterinarian

mail carrier

Where does the story happen?

community

Reading Strategy | **Prior Knowledge**

Prior knowledge is what you already know about a topic. As you read, think about the topics that you already know something about.

People Can Help

On Your Own

by Lawrence Po

illustrated by Apryl Stott and Sue Miller

Dot can help Ned send a letter.

Sal can help Mom and Tam.

She can take Mom and Tam

on the bus.

Ed can sit at a desk.

He can help get a book
about a cat.

Dan is sad about
his dog, Top.

Nan can help Top.

Tom can help Tim, Pam,
and Ted cross.
A lot of people can help.

Read the questions. Say the answers.
Use Sight Words and Story Words.

1. What does Ned give Dot?
2. How does Sal help Mom and Tam?
3. Why is Dan sad?
4. Who can help you in your community?

Reading Strategy	Prior Knowledge
How did using what you know help you read?	

31–32

Grammar and Writing

Can + Verb

Use ***can*** + verb to talk about things people are able to do.

I **can** play soccer.

Use ***can*** + ***not*** + verb for things people are not able to do.

He **can't** swim.

cannot → **can't**

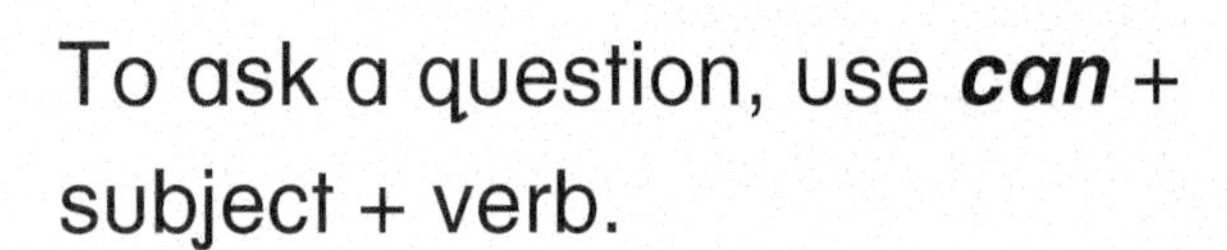

To ask a question, use ***can*** + subject + verb.

Can he skateboard? Yes, he **can**.

Practice A

Write *can* or *can't* in the blank.

1. I ____can____ swing.

2. He ____________ run.

3. They ____________ play soccer.

4. She ____________ play basketball.

Practice B

Write *can* or *can't* in the blank.

1. Can you run? Yes, I can.
2. ________ you swim? Yes, I ________.
3. ________ he skate? No, he ________.
4. ________ she sing? No, she ________.
5. ________ they ski? No, they ________.

Apply

Example: A: Can you play soccer?

B: Yes, I can.

Can you swim?
Can you run?
Can you skate?

Write

Draw a picture of things you can do.
Write about them.

I can swim. I can play soccer.
I can skateboard.

WB 33–34

Vocabulary

These words will help you understand the reading.

Words to Know

1. Look at the man in back.

2. He passes to another man.

3. This glass of milk is a delicious snack.

Sight Words

look

the

another

Story Words

delicious

snack

Your Turn

Pick a word from either box.

Use the word in a sentence.

Ask your teacher for help.

35

Phonics

Short *u*; *b*, *j*

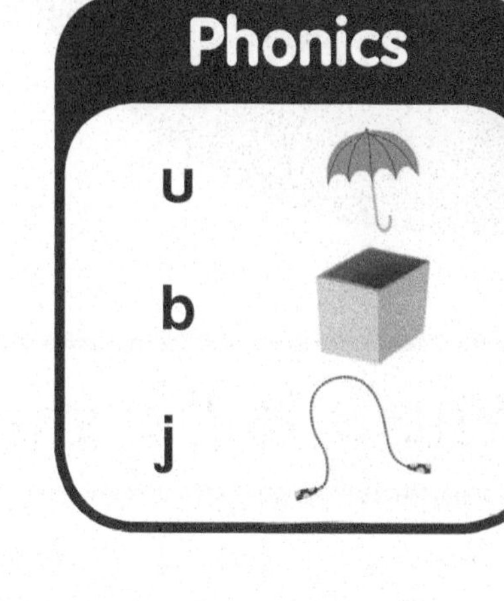

Look at each picture and word.
Listen to the letter sounds.
Say the word.

jam

bus

up

bug

36

Your Turn

Which letter stands for the missing sound?

__ u g

c __ p

__ e d

Story Preview

Bud

Dad

Who is in the story?

Pat

Where does the story happen?

shops

Reading Strategy | Main Idea

What is the most important idea in the story? It is the main idea. As you read, look for the main idea.

Reading 2

Bud and His Dad

On Your Own

by Denise Lewis
illustrated by Barbara Spurll

Bud and his dad can

hop to the shop.

Bud can have milk and
jam. Bud likes milk and jam
a lot. Mmmm.

Bud and his dad hop to
another shop.

Bud and his dad see Pat.
Bud can have another snack.
Mmmm. Mmmm.

Look! A blue snack is on Bud.

Mmmm, it is delicious!

Read the questions. Say the answers.
Use Sight Words and Story Words.

1. Where do Bud and his dad hop?
2. What do Bud and his dad buy?
3. Who do they see in another shop?
4. Why are shops important?

Speaking Tip

Look at the pictures again. Retell the story. This will help you learn new words.

Reading Strategy | **Main Idea**

How did understanding the main idea help you read?

37–38

Grammar and Writing

Possessives

The possessive adjectives ***my, your, her, his, their,*** and ***our*** show who owns something.

I	→	**my**	it	→	**its**
he	→	**his**	we	→	**our**
she	→	**her**	they	→	**their**

This is **my** mom.

You can also use: name + apostrophe (') + ***s***.

This is **Maria's** kite.

Practice A

Complete each sentence with the correct possessive adjective.

1. This is ___her___ room. (she)
2. This is ________ cover. (it)
3. That is ________ home. (we)
4. This is ________ new bike. (I)
5. He is ________ dad. (they)
6. She is ________ mom. (he)

Practice B

Fill in the blank with the name + 's.

1. That is ___Anna's___ doll. (Anna)
2. Do you have ______________ pencil? (Jun)
3. This is ______________ backpack. (Diego)
4. That is ______________ book. (Pierre)

Is that your paper?
Is that your pen?
Is that your pencil?

Apply

Example: A: Is that your book?

B: No, it isn't. It's Jin's book.

Write

Draw a picture of something that belongs to a friend. Write about it.

This is Jed's bike.
His bike is new.
It is red.

39–40

Vocabulary

Words to Know

These words will help you understand the reading.

1. I can use this pen.

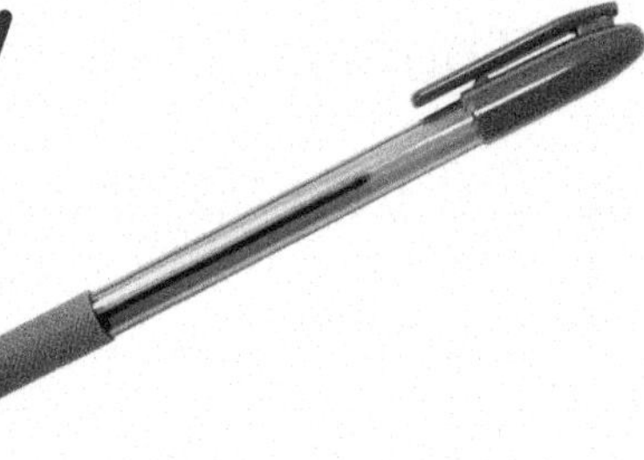

2. School can be fun.

3. The doctor got a package today.

Sight Words

- use
- this
- be

Story Words

- doctor
- package

Your Turn

Pick a word from either box.

Use the word in a sentence.

WB 41

Phonics

Long *a*; *r*, *w*

Look at each picture and word.

Listen to the letter sounds.

Say the word.

Your Turn

Sound out the words. Point to the word for the picture.

wade **made**

take **rake**

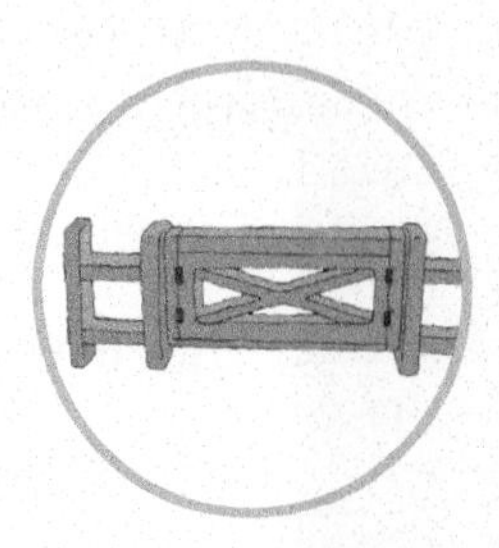

gate **get**

Story Preview

What is the story about?

The story is about Joe.
Joe brings packages to people.

Reading Strategy	Sequence

Sequence tells when things happen in order. What is the sequence of this story? As you read, put the events in order to help you understand the story.

Reading 3

Joe Has a Job

On Your Own

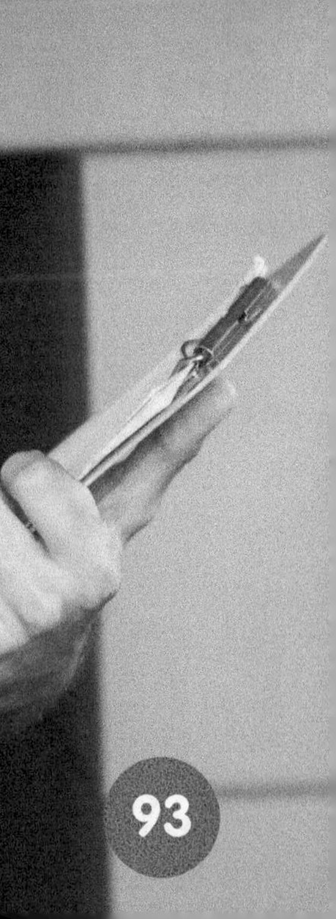

Joe has a job.

The packages will not be late.

Joe will put this package on the cart.

Joe can hand a package to Doctor Rose.
Doctor Rose helps pets get well.

The package has medicine.
Doctor Rose can use it.
It will help sick cats and dogs.

Joe has a package for Sam.
Her grandma sent it. It's Sam's birthday!

Think It Over

Read the questions. Say the answers.
Use Sight Words and Story Words.

1. Who is Joe?
2. What does Joe deliver to Doctor Rose?
3. What does Doctor Rose do?
4. Why do people send packages?

Reading Strategy	Sequence
How did thinking about sequence help you understand the story?	

43–44

A CLOSER LOOK AT...

Sending a Package

Nate can send a package.

Jim can load it in the van.

The package gets sorted.

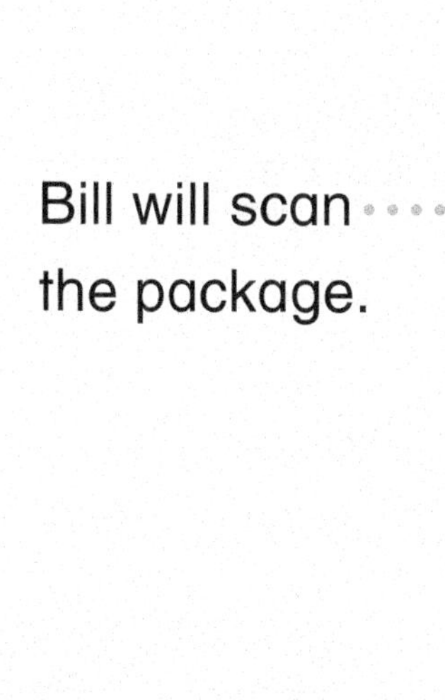

Bill will scan the package.

Pat will get the package from Nate.

Activity to Do

Choose a classmate to deliver a package. Choose something to send. Write a note. Say who it is for and who it is from. Give your package to the classmate for delivery.

Grammar and Writing

Will + Verb

Use ***will*** and future time words to talk about the future. Examples of time words are *tonight, tomorrow, next week*.

Use ***will not*** + verb for what you think will not happen in the future.

It **will rain** tomorrow. It **will not be** sunny.

To ask a question, use ***will*** + subject + verb.

Will you **call** your friend tonight? **No, I won't.**

will not → **won't**

Practice A

Fill in the blank with *will* or *won't*.

1. The family ___will___ get mail this afternoon.
2. She __________ jump soon.
3. I think he __________ win the race.
4. They __________ do their homework tonight.
5. He __________ finish the game.

Practice B

Answer the questions. Write the sentences in your notebook.

1. What will you do after school?
2. What will you not do after school?

Apply

Example: A: Will you see a friend today?
B: Yes, I will.

do homework
go to the park
watch a movie

Write

This boy just missed the bus. What will happen?

He will be mad.
He will be late.
He will get in trouble.

45–46

Put It All Together

Projects

Your teacher will help you choose one of these projects.

Written 

Write about a person in your community.

What is his or her name?

What job does he or she do?

Write about this person and his or her job.

THE BIG QUESTION

Who are the people who help in your community? Talk about it.

Oral

Interview a person in your community.

Interview someone who works in your community.

Ask: *Do you like your job? Why do you like your job?*

Visual/Active

When I grow up...

What job in your community would you like to have? Act out how you would do that job.

Listening and Speaking Workshop

Tell a Story about a Fun Thing You Do

Tell the class a story about a fun thing you do.

① Prepare

Tell a story about what you do for fun. Write four sentences about it.

② Practice and Present

Practice with a partner. Then tell your story to the class.

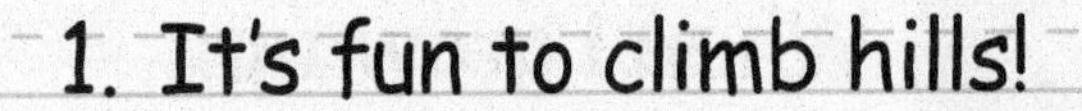

1. It's fun to climb hills!
2. I can climb the big hill in the park.
3. I climb the hill after school.
4. It's fun because I can see everyone from the top of the hill.

Useful Language

Listen and repeat.

- I can play / run / swim.
- It's fun because . . .
- I do it with my friend / dad.

As you speak, do this:

- Use your voice, hands, and facial expressions to tell story.
- Show your feelings. Say a sentence that ends with a *!*.

Listening Tip

Listen to your teacher. Learn the expression *have fun*. How do you have fun?

As you listen, do this:

- Look at the speaker. Ask questions if you don't understand.
- Listen for words you learned. How does this help you understand what people say?
- Think about what you learn from people's words, faces, and hands. How can you get clues about hidden ideas or information?

3 Evaluate

Ask yourself these questions:

- How well did you understand the directions?
- How did you use your voice, hands, and face to tell the story?

Speaking Tip

Stand up straight, look at your audience, and smile when you make your presentation.

Writing Workshop

Write a Letter

You will write a letter to a friend.

① **Prewrite** List the things you will do after school. Look at Ho's list.

October 3

Dear Chang,

Today I will:

1. look for my ball and bat
2. go to the park
3. play baseball with Peter
4. eat ice cream

Your friend,

Ho

② **Draft** Write a letter. Use the ideas in your list. Use new words from the unit.

3 **Revise** Read your letter. Use the Revising Checklist to make your writing better.

Revising Checklist

- ✔ Did I tell the date?
- ✔ Did I write the person's name on the letter?
- ✔ Did I include details about my plans?

December 10

Dear Chang,

How are you? After school I will get my ~~basball~~ baseball and bat. Then I will go to the park with my ~~frend~~ friend Peter. We will play baseball. Then we will eat ice cream at his house.

Your friend,

Ho

4. **Edit** Trade papers. Correct your partner's letter. Use the Editing Checklist.

5. **Publish** Make a clean copy of your letter. Share it with the class.

Editing Checklist

- ✔ Each sentence starts with a capital.
- ✔ Each sentence ends with a period.
- ✔ Possessive words are correct (*my, Anna's*).

Spelling Tip

You learned the long *a* sound before. When the word or syllable ends in *e*, the *a* sound is long.

plate

baseball

WB 49–50

Fluency

For Each Reading...

1. Listen to the sentences.
2. Listen and use your finger to follow the words.
3. Listen, use your finger, and say the words.

Sal can help Mom and Tam.

People Can Help

Bud can have milk and jam.

Bud and His Dad

Joe can hand a package to
Doctor Rose.

Joe Has a Job

51–52

Unit 3

Traditions

People celebrate traditions. Street festivals are popular in many cultures. Tell the class about a tradition in your family.

THE BIG QUESTION

What is your favorite way to celebrate?

View and Respond

Watch the video. What is it about?

Talk about the poster. What do you see?

Visit Pearson English Portal.

Build Unit Background

What Do You Know about Traditions?

Use what you know.

People follow traditions.

A Thanksgiving parade is a tradition.

On Valentine's Day, people give cards to each other.

At this Cherry Blossom Festival, families have picnics.

Your Turn

Think about your favorite tradition. Tell the class about it.

Build Unit Background

Sing about Traditions

Family Traditions Song

Family, family, get together.

Time to celebrate, all together.

We meet and greet.

What will you say?

Gather around.

And let us play.

Family, family, get together.

Time to celebrate, all together.

We will eat.

What will you bring?

Gather round

And let us sing.

Family, family, get together.

Time to celebrate, all together.

Reading Tip

We read English from left to right and top to bottom.

Vocabulary

These words will help you understand the reading.

Words to Know

1. Lots of people play at birthday parties.

2. I like to play, too.

3. I like green balloons best.

4. A carnival is a celebration.

5. People can wear a costume.

Sight Words

of
to
green

Story Words

carnival
celebration
costume

Your Turn

Pick one word from either box.
Use the word in a sentence.
Ask your teacher for help.

WB 55

Phonics

Long *i*; *v*, *x*

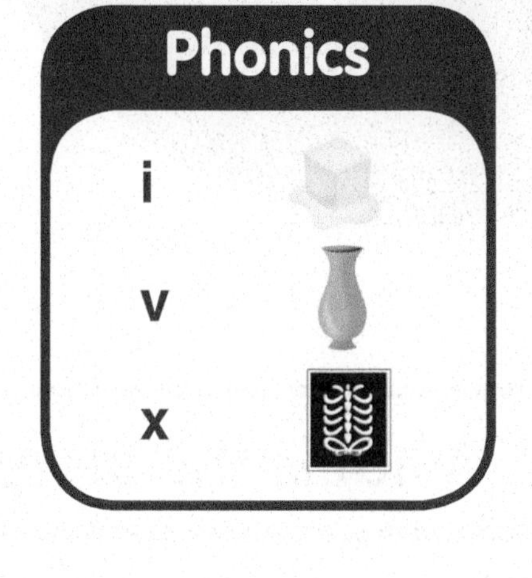

Look at each picture and word.

Listen to the letter sounds.

Say the word.

van

ox

five

ride

Your Turn

Complete each word with the missing letter.

b __ ke

w __ ve

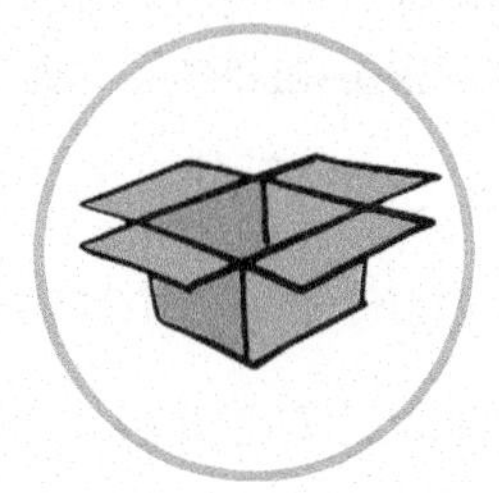

b __ x

k __ te

Story Preview

China

What is the story about?

Ghana

United States

Brazil

The story is about celebrations around the world.

Reading Strategy | **Use Pictures**

Looking carefully at the pictures can help you better understand the story. As you read, look at the pictures to see what each page is about.

Celebration Time!

On Your Own

Reading 1

by Carol Johnson

I am having lots and lots of fun!
It is celebration time!

It's the New Year. It can be named for an ox, rat, or ram. Around the world, it is celebration time!

I can have a fun time at
a carnival.
I can put on a big blue wig
and a mask to hide.

I can smile and dress up.
I can dress up in a red
and green costume.
It is fun to dress up in a hat.

On July 4, I can dress up
in red, white, and blue.
I can wave a flag.

Mom, Dad, and I are gazing at the sky.
Pop! Pop! Pop! Pop! Pop! Pop!

In Ghana, tribes plant crops.
It is celebration time.
Lots of drums go tap, tap, tap!

Think It Over

Read the questions. Say the answers.
Use Sight Words and Story Words.

1. What can the New Year be named for?
2. Why do people like to dress up for celebrations?
3. How are some celebrations the same? How are they different?
4. How does your family have celebrations?

Reading Strategy	Use Pictures

How did looking at the pictures help you understand the story?

57–58

A CLOSER LOOK AT... Celebrations

China

In China, people dress in dragon costumes to celebrate the New Year.

Brazil

In Brazil, people celebrate Carnival with feasts and parades for days and days.

United States

In the United States, people celebrate Independence Day with fireworks.

Ghana

In Ghana, Djembe drummers perform at celebrations.

Activity to Do

On Flag Day we celebrate our flag.

- Draw and color your country's flag.
- Write a story about your flag.
- Show your drawing. Tell your story to the class.

Grammar and Writing

Verbs with *-ing*

Use verbs with ***-ing*** to talk about things you are doing now.

I am **reading**. She is **laughing**. They are **talking**.

Use ***am, is,*** or ***are*** before the verb in a statement.

I **am** climbing. She **is** swinging. They **are** eating.

To make a question, start with ***What am, is,*** or ***are,*** then the subject, and then the verb.

What am I doing? **What is** she doing? **What are** they doing?

Practice A

Use *am, is,* or *are* to fill in the blank.

1. I ___am___ eating rice.
2. He ________ kicking the ball.
3. You ________ sleeping in bed.
4. The girls ________ listening to music.

Grammar Tip

Use *am* with *I*. Use *is* with *he* or *she*. Use *are* with *you, they,* and *we*.

Practice B

Fill in the blanks with *am, is,* or *are* and the verb in parentheses + *ing.*

1. (walk) He is walking down the street.
2. (wash) They ______________ their clothes.
3. (fish) I ______________ in the pond.
4. (drink) You ______________ lemonade.
5. (play) She ______________ in the grass.

Apply

Choose an activity from the box to act out. Then have your partner guess what you're doing.

Example: A: What am I doing?

B: You're jumping rope.

Write

Draw a picture of you doing your favorite activity. Write about your picture.

I'm playing baseball. I am throwing the ball. My friend is catching the ball.

59–60

Vocabulary

These words will help you understand the reading.

Sight Words

first
then
with

Story Words

envelopes
dragon
parade

Words to Know

1. First they got red envelopes.

2. Then they took a ride with friends.

3. They saw the dragons dancing.

4. The parade was so much fun!

Your Turn

Pick one word from either box.

Use the word in a sentence.

61

Phonics

Long *u*; *k*, *ck*

Look at each picture and word.

Listen to the letter sounds.

Say the word.

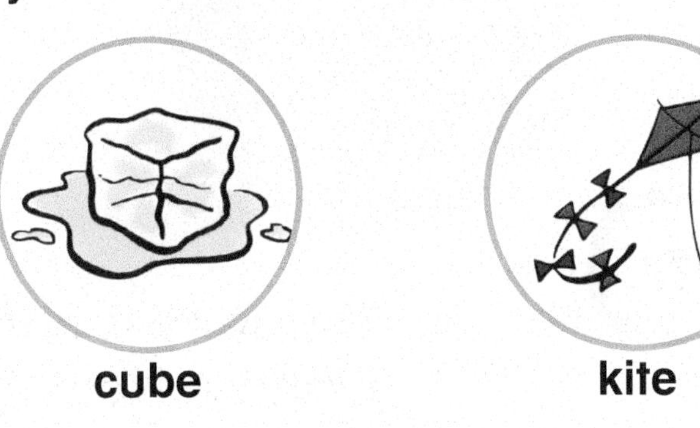

cube **kite**

duck

Your Turn

Sound out the words. Point to the word for the picture.

use us up

kit kick kite

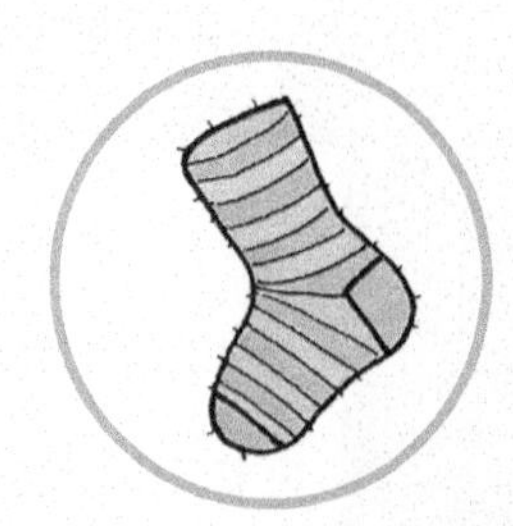

sock sob spot

Story Preview

Reading Tip

As you read, write down answers to *What, When,* and *Where.*

What is the story about?

The story is about Chinese New Year. Chinese New Year is a celebration.

Reading Strategy | **Summarize**

When you summarize, you tell the most important information in a story or poem. As you read, find the important information.

Reading 2

Chinese New Year

Every year people say, "Hooray!"

Because the Chinese New Year lasts for 15 days.

First, it's time for the family to eat.
Sweet rice cakes are a great treat!

Next, Chen gives Kai a sweet snack, and then Kai gives him one back.

Then Grandma gives them envelopes
that are red.
"There are coins inside!" they said.

Look at the cute dragon the children made.
They bring it with them to the parade.

At the parade they see dragons and lions dancing.

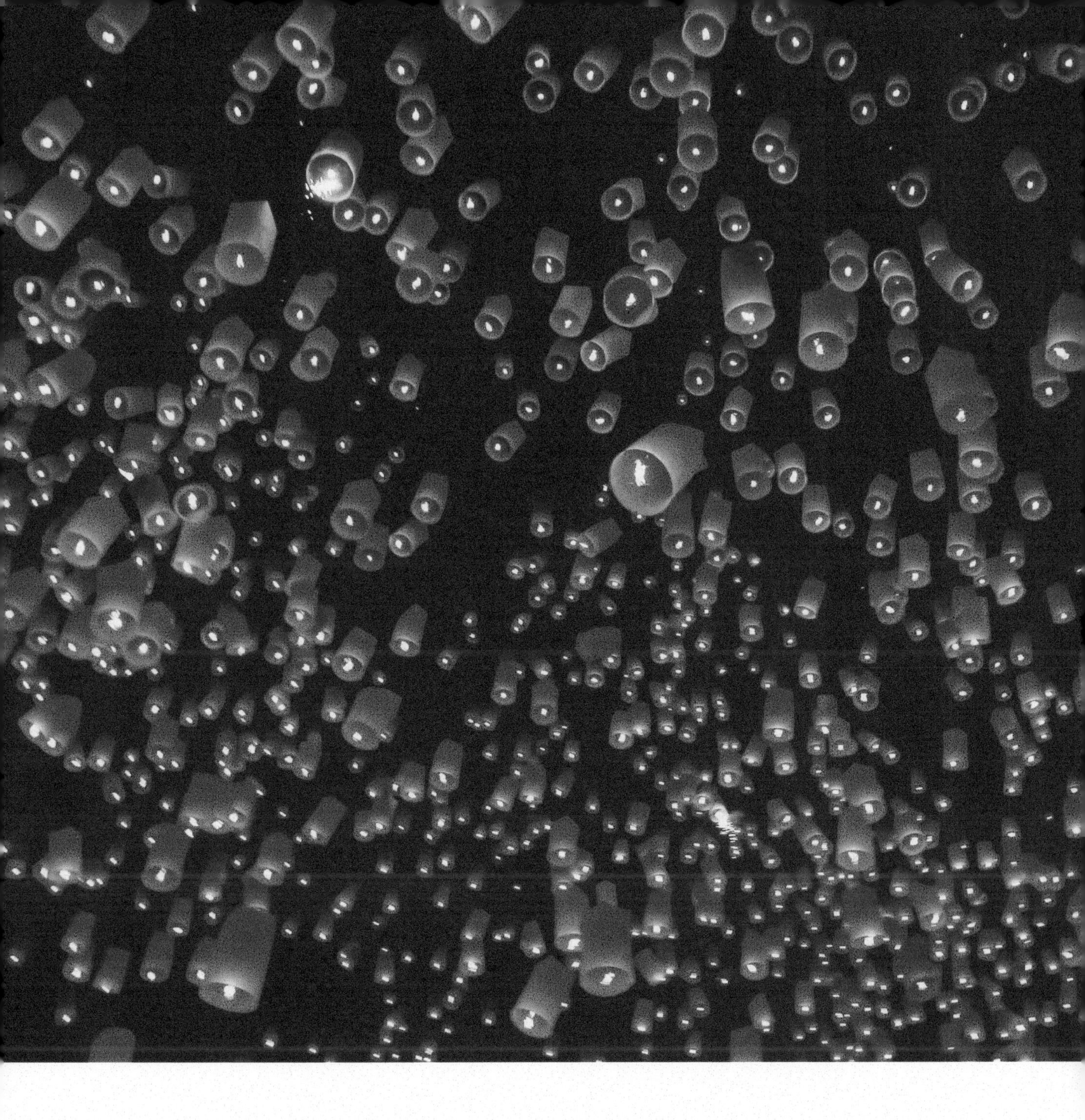

On the fifteenth day, they look up in the night sky to see lots of lights passing by.

Finally, the Chinese New Year is done.
Everyone is tired but had lots of fun.

Think It Over

Read the questions. Say the answers.
Use Sight Words and Story Words.

1. How long does the Chinese New Year last?
2. What are some fun things the family does to celebrate?
3. What does Grandma give the kids?
4. What do they see at the parade?

Reading Strategy	Summarize
Use your notes to summarize the story with a partner.	

63–64

Grammar and Writing

Adjectives

An adjective describes a noun or a pronoun.
An adjective can come before a noun.

I see a **green** frog. This frog has **big** eyes.

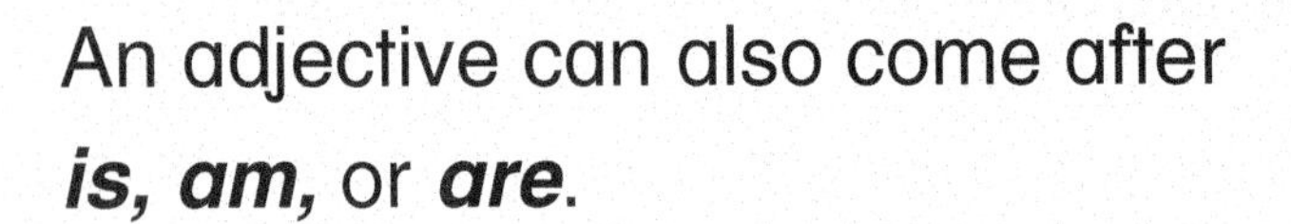

An adjective can also come after ***is, am,*** or ***are***.

The dog **is** small. My shoes **are** black.

Practice A

Put the words in order so they make sense.

1. tall/I/am I am tall.
2. They/have/cat/a big ____________.
3. Is/loud/her music ____________?
4. nice/You/are ____________.
5. hat/a black/see/I ____________.

Practice B

Complete each sentence with *is*, *am*, or *are* and an adjective from the box.

pretty, blue, tall, little, soft

1. My eyes are blue.
2. The building ____________.
3. I ____________.
4. The pillows ____________.
5. The flower ____________.

Apply

Ask questions with *What color is* or *What color are*.

Example: A: What color are your eyes?

B: They're brown.

Write

Draw a picture of you. Describe yourself.

I have brown eyes.

My hair is brown. It is long.

Vocabulary

These words will help you understand the reading.

Words to Know

1. A country's flag is a symbol.

2. People live and work in their community.

3. The American flag is red, white, and blue.

4. What does our flag look like?

Sight Words

- white
- blue
- our

Story Words

- symbol
- country
- community

Your Turn

Pick one word from either box.

Use the word in a sentence.

Phonics

Long *o; g, z*

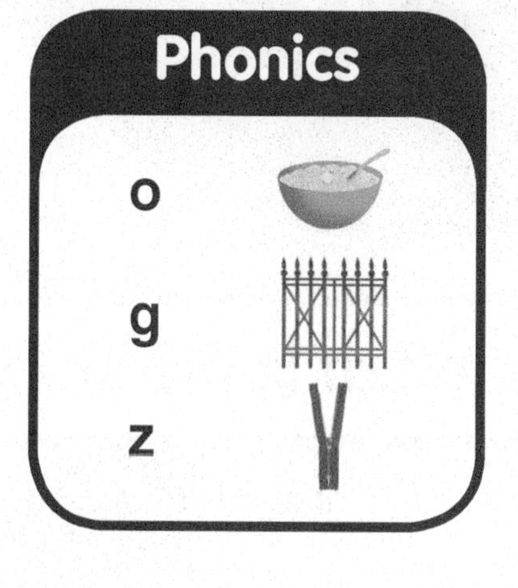

Look at each picture and word.

Listen to the letter sounds.

Say the word.

gate

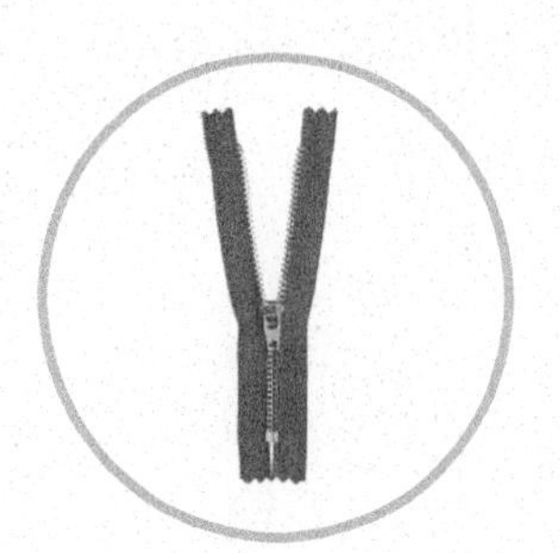

zip

stove

hole

68

Your Turn

Which letter stands for the sound in the beginning of the word?

g n z

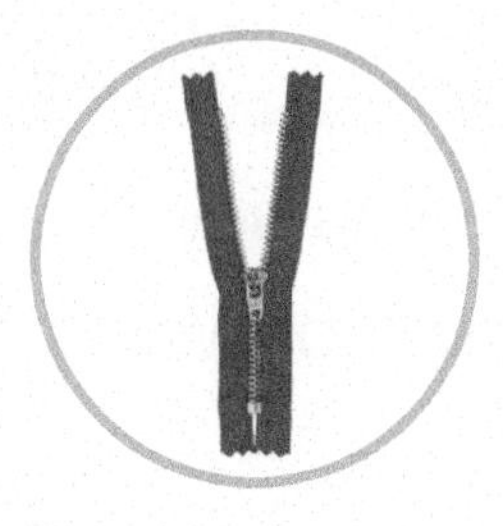

g c z

o g z

o t g

Story Preview

What is the story about?

The story is about flags.

Reading Strategy | **Visualizing**

Visualizing is the pictures you see in your head while you read. As you read, look for words that help you visualize the story.

Reading 3

A Flag

On Your Own

A flag is a symbol of a country.
It shows that we belong to a community.

I see a flag at our school.
It has a black stripe, a red stripe, and a yellow stripe.

I see a flag at the soccer game.
It is green, yellow, and blue.
It has 27 white stars.

I see a flag at the zoo.
It is red, white, and blue.

There is even an Olympic flag!
It has 5 colored rings.

I see a blue ring, a yellow ring, a black ring, a green ring, and a red ring.

Flags are seen in lots of places. Look around. Do you see your country's flag?

Think It Over

Read the questions. Say the answers.
Use Sight Words and Story Words.

1. What does a flag symbolize?
2. What does the flag at the soccer game look like?
3. What colors are the rings on the Olympic flag?
4. Describe what your country's flag looks like.

Reading Strategy	Visualizing
How did visualizing help you understand the story?	

WB 69–70

Grammar and Writing

Simple Present Tense: Statements

Use the simple present for things that happen often or don't change.

I **go** to bed at eight o'clock.

For ***he, she,*** and ***it,*** add ***-s*** after the verb.

She **plays** outside after school.

For ***I, you, we,*** and ***they,*** use the base form of a verb.

I **get** up at 6 every morning.

To make a negative sentence, use ***does*** or ***do*** + ***not***.

He **does not** like apples. They **do not** live in my neighborhood.

Practice A

Fill in the blank with the correct present tense form of the verb.

1. (sleep) She ________________ late.

2. (eat) They ________________ fish.

3. (walk) He ________________ to work.

Practice B

Fill in the blank with either *do not* or *does not*.

1. They ___do not___ talk in the library.
2. She ______________ like the color orange.
3. I ______________ eat sugar.
4. We ______________ watch TV on school nights.
5. He ______________ fight with his brother.

Apply

Talk with a partner about things you do during your school vacation. Have your partner agree or disagree.

Example: A: During school vacation, I go to the beach.
B: Me, too.

Write

Draw a picture of things you do and do not do in school. Describe them.

In school, I read. I write, too.
I do not sleep.

Put It All Together

Projects

Your teacher will help you choose one of these projects.

Written 

Write about a family celebration.

What do you do? Who is there? Write about it.

THE BIG QUESTION

What is your favorite way to celebrate? Talk about it.

Oral

Describe a family celebration.

Without saying what the celebration is, describe it. Can your class guess what your family celebration is?

Visual/Active

Draw a picture of a family celebration.

Draw a picture that shows your family celebrating.

Listening and Speaking Workshop

Description Guessing Game

GO 12

Play this game to practice describing animals.

Useful Language

Listen and repeat.

- My animal is (small and blue).
- My animal can (fly).
- My animal lives in (a forest).
- It eats (worms).

1 Prepare

Choose three animals. Draw a picture of each animal. For each animal, write words in a word web. See the word web below with *bird* as an example.

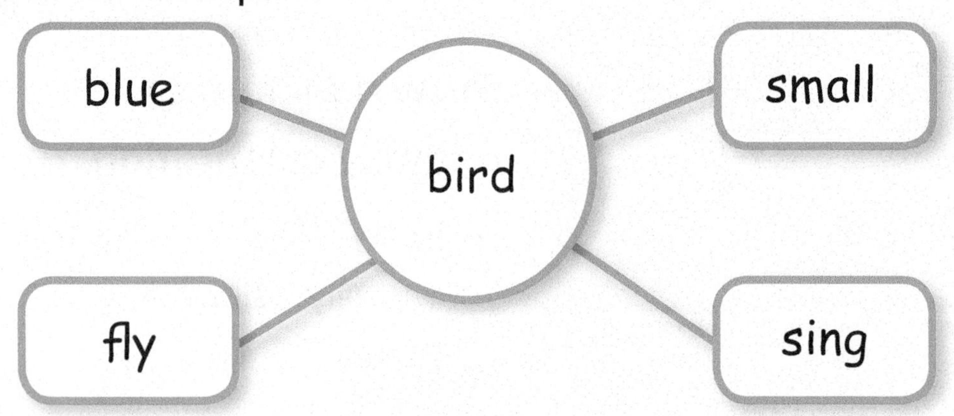

2 Practice and Present

Don't let your classmates see your pictures. When it's your turn, use your words to describe an animal. Who can guess what the animal is? When someone guesses correctly, hold up your picture. Then the winner takes a turn.

As you speak, do this:

- Use short and long sentences.
- Have fun. Remember, this is a game.

As you listen, do this:

- Take notes in your notebook.
- Listen for words you know.
- If an idea or information is not clear, listen for clues. Think again.
- Think about what you know about the animals.

3 Evaluate

- Did you choose good words to describe your animals?
- How well did you understand the rules?

More Practice

Choose a picture of an animal you don't know. Your partner listens as you describe it.

- Don't show the picture.
- Tell the most important thing and two details about the animal.
- Ask your partner to guess what it is.
- Your partner can repeat the same steps with you.

Writing Workshop

Write a Descriptive Paragraph

A descriptive paragraph tells about a person or place.

① **Prewrite** First, think about a place you like. How does it look? How does it feel? What do you do there? Then draw a web and write in it.

Ana wrote in her web.

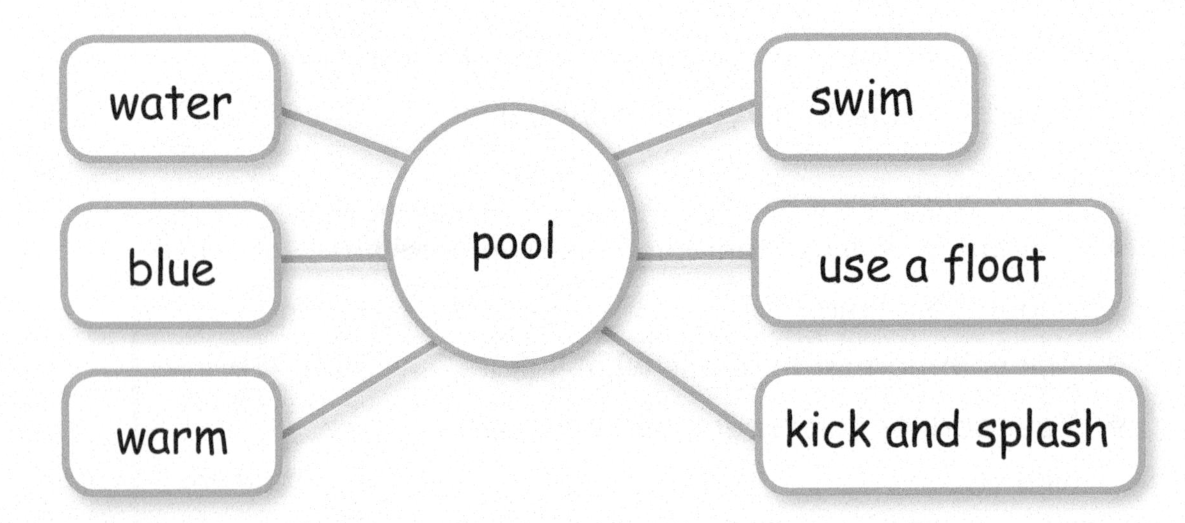

2 **Draft** Write a descriptive paragraph. Use the ideas in your web. Use new words from the unit.

3 **Revise** Read your paragraph. Use the Revising Checklist to make it better.

Here is Ana's descriptive paragraph.

I like the pool. The pool is big
and the water is ~~blu~~ blue and warm.
My sister and I swim in the water.
We throw the ~~bal~~ ball and kick
and splash.

Revising Checklist

- ✔ I used simple present tense verbs correctly.
- ✔ I used adjectives correctly.

④ **Edit** Trade papers. Correct your partner's paragraph. Use the Editing Checklist.

⑤ **Publish** Make a clean copy of your paragraph. Share it with the class.

Spelling Tip

When a short word ends in *l*, *f*, or *s*, you often double the last letters: ball, puff, less.

Editing Checklist

- ✔ The subjects and verbs agree.
- ✔ Pronouns agree with verbs.
- ✔ Verb tenses are correct.

WB 75–76

Fluency

For Each Reading...

1. Listen to the sentences.
2. Listen and use your finger to follow the words.
3. Listen, use your finger, and say the words.

I can have lots and lots of fun!

Celebration Time

They bring it with them to the parade.

Chinese New Year

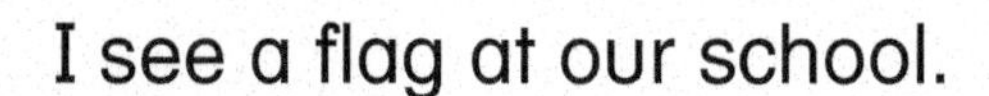

I see a flag at our school.

A Flag

77–78

Unit 4

Animals and Plants

Some plants help animals. Some animals help plants. Living things can help each other. Tell about how living things help each other.

THE BIG QUESTION

How can living things help each other?

View and Respond

Watch the video. What is it about?

Talk about the poster. What do you see?

Visit Pearson English Portal.

Build Unit Background

What Do You Know about Animals and Plants?

Use what you know.

I can eat some plants.

We can use trees
to make this home.

Plants and animals can help each other.

People can help plants and animals, too.

Animals can be our friends!

Your Turn

What kind of pet would you like to have? Tell the class about it.

Build Unit Background

Sing about Animals and Plants

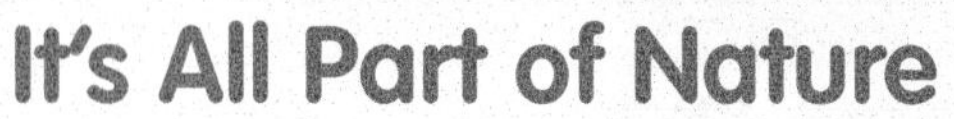

It's All Part of Nature

Frogs and bees and turtles
and fleas,
Lions, bats, and weasels.
Cats and crows, everyone knows,
Are all part of nature!

Trees and grasses across
the land,
Growing ever stronger.
A lovely rose, I bet you know,
Is all part of nature!

Vocabulary

These words will help you understand the reading.

Words to Know

1. Why can I see the bird? It is because I look at it with my binoculars.

2. The eagle flies so gracefully out in the clear blue sky.

Sight Words

why
because
so
out

Story Words

waddle
duckling
feathers

3. All the ducks waddle along together.
4. A baby duck is called a duckling.

5. Duck feathers are very soft.

Your Turn

Pick one word from either box.

Use the word in a sentence.

Work with a partner.

81

Phonics

Long *e; ch, sh*

Look at each picture and word. Listen to the letter sounds. Say the word.

chick **ship**

read

Your Turn

Which letter, or letters, stand for the sound at the beginning of the word?

ch th sh

ch sh dr

a e i o

Story Preview

Reading Tip

You can use the pictures in the story to guess what will happen.

Who is in the story?

duckling

duck

Where does the story happen?

pond

Reading Strategy | **Predict**

You can guess, or predict, what will happen in a story. Use what you know and the clues in the story. As you read, try to predict what might happen.

Little Duck

by Sarah Beacker

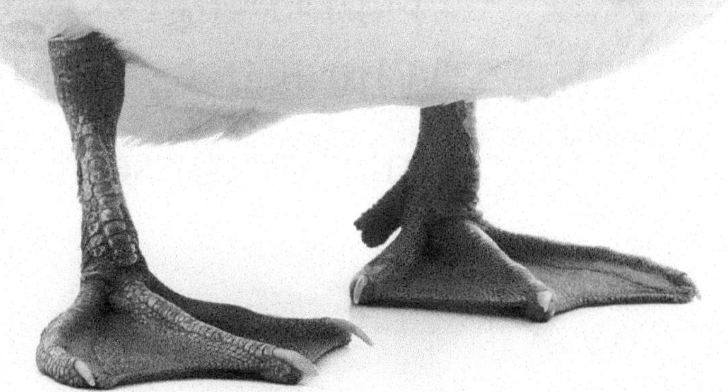

Peep! Peep! Peep! I see a duck. Why is it so small? It is so small because it just hatched.

An egg shell cracks. I see feet!
I see a beak! A duckling can get
out of its shell.

A duckling came out of an egg.
It is a cute duckling. But it can
not stand up yet.

Ducks can walk. Ducks waddle and sway to walk. A duck says, "Peep! Peep! Peep!"

Ducks check for bugs. Why?
Ducks check for bugs because
ducks like to eat bugs.

Three ducks swim in a big pond. Ducks can swim. Ducks kick big, flat feet to swim.

A duck has feathers so it
will not get cold.
Little ducks get big fast!

Think It Over

Read the questions. Say the answers.
Use Sight Words and Story Words.

1. What does the duckling say?
2. Why is the duckling so small?
3. How do ducks swim?
4. Compare a duck to a chicken.

Reading Tip

To help you understand the story, ask a partner a question about it.

Reading Strategy	Predict
How does predicting help you understand the story?	

83–84

Grammar and Writing

Simple Present Tense: Questions

To make questions with the simple present tense, use ***what, when,*** and ***where*** + ***do/does*** + subject + **verb**.

Where do you go on the weekend?
I go to the store with my parents.
What do you ask them to buy?
I ask for my favorite food and drinks.

When does Julio spend time with his grandpa?
After school.
What does Julio do with his grandpa after school?
He reads and plays video games with his grandpa.

Practice A

Use *do* or *does* to fill in the blanks.

1. What <u>does</u> she do at home?
2. What ______ he do after school?
3. When ______ you do your homework?
4. Where ______ they go on the weekend?
5. When ______ she spend time with her mom?

Practice B

Circle *do* or *does* to make the sentences correct.

1. What do / does she do / does on the weekend?
2. When do / does you do / does your practices?
3. Where do / does you do / does your homework?
4. What do / does they do / does for lunch?

Apply

Choose a question from the box to ask your partner. Then have your partner answer you.

Example: A: What do you do after school?

B: I watch TV.

- When do you do your homework?
- What does your family do on the weekends?

Write

Write about the things you do after school.

First, I do my homework. Next, I play soccer. Then I have dinner.

WB 85–86

Reading 2
Prepare to Read

Vocabulary

These words will help you understand the reading.

Words to Know

1. **Before** a plant can **grow**, it needs sunlight.

2. **After** sunlight, a plant needs water, too.

3. The boy adds **water** to his plant. Then a **blossom** will bloom.

4. I like picking pumpkins in a **pumpkin** patch.

Sight Words

before
grow
after

Story Words

water
blossom
pumpkin

Your Turn

Pick one word from either box.
Use the word in a sentence.

87

Phonics

Long *a*; *th*, *y*

Look at each picture and word. Listen to the letter sounds. Say the word.

Your Turn

Sound out the words. Point to the word for the picture.

snail snake

play pail

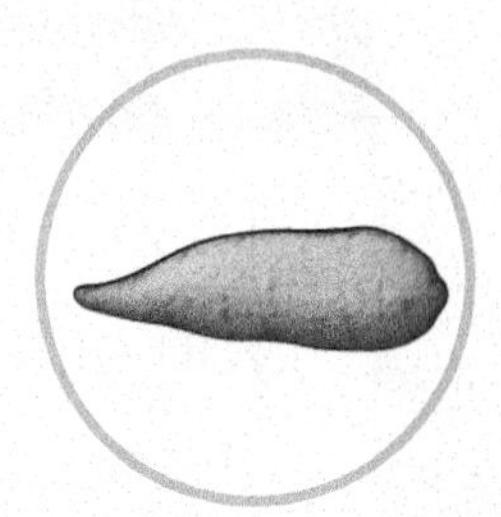

yam yak

Story Preview

seeds

peaches

leaves

carrot

What is in the story?

watermelon

pumpkin

flowers

What is the story about?

The story is about all kinds of plants.

Reading Strategy | **Use Prior Knowledge**

To improve your understanding of a story, use what you already know. As you read, think of what you already know about the topics in the story.

Plants

On Your Own

Reading 2

by Nikki Pagano
illustrated by
Linda Holt Ayriss

Seeds make plants. A seed needs a lot of rain and a lot of sun before it can grow big and strong.

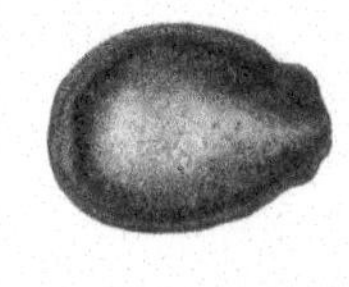

You may plant this black seed in wet dirt. After about six days, vines will pop out. Next, a blossom may bloom. Then watermelons may grow.

A watermelon is red and green. If you wait, it will get big and sweet. Yum! Yum! Yum!

This seed is named a pit or a stone. It may grow to be a peach. It will need a lot of water and sun to help it grow.

A peach grows on a tree. Can you see big, green leaves on this peach tree? Pick a peach off a tree. A peach is a sweet treat that tastes fine.
Yum! Yum! Yum! Yum!

Do you see the thin seeds? First you add water and sun to these seeds.

Then a big orange pumpkin will grow.
It will lay on the soft ground.

Pumpkins have thin lines and thick stems. Pumpkins have seeds inside. You may make pumpkins into pie. Mmmmm. Yum! Yum! Yum! Yum!

Think It Over

Read the questions. Say the answers.
Use Sight Words and Story Words.

1. What does a seed need to grow?
2. What happens to the watermelon seed after six days?
3. What do we call the seed of a peach?
4. Why are plants important?

Speaking Tip

Speak slowly and clearly.

Reading Strategy | **Use Prior Knowledge**

Did you understand the story better because you already knew something about the topics in the story?

WB

A CLOSER LOOK AT... Plants

Carrot

Can you see the parts of a carrot? Name all of its parts.

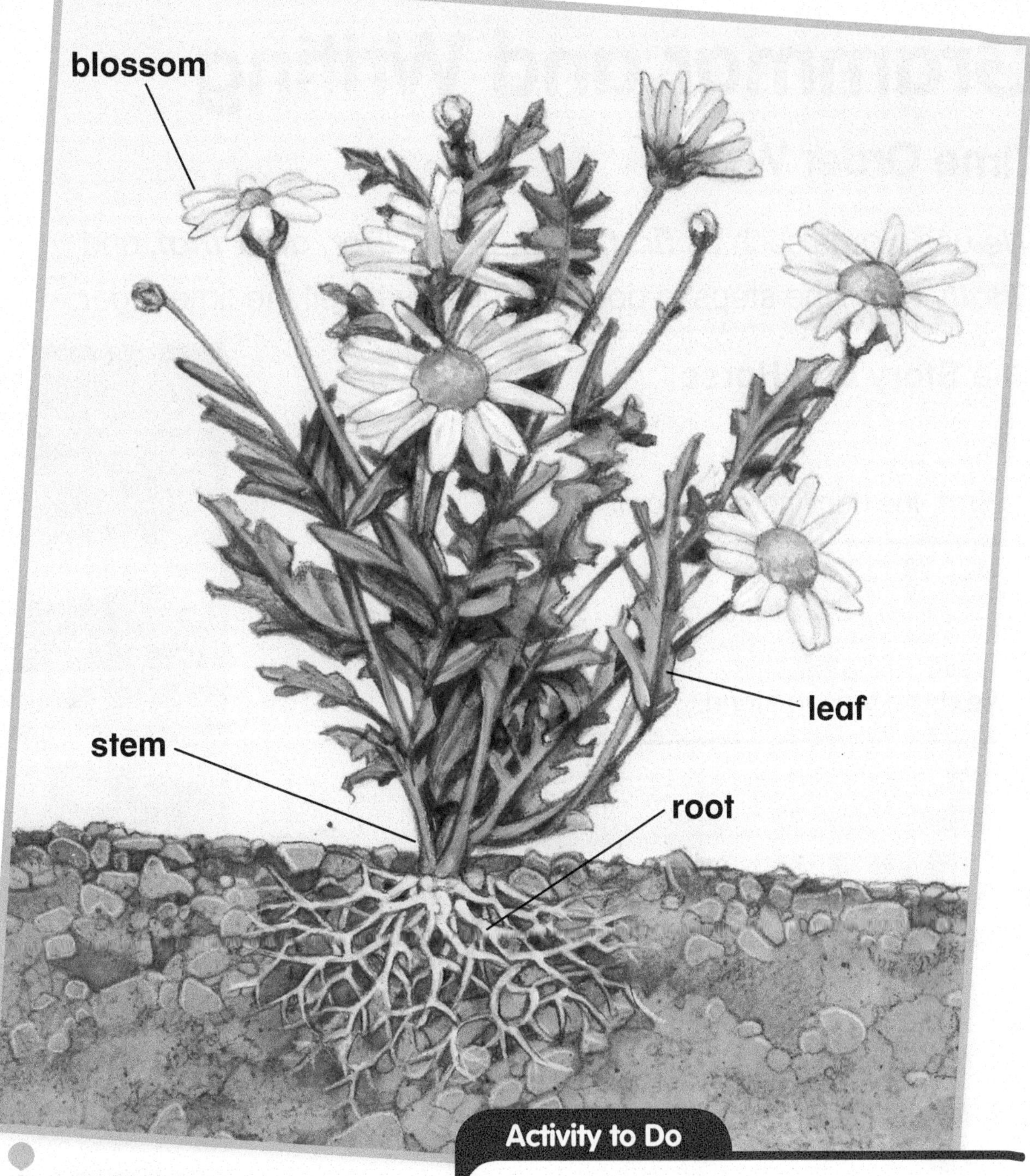

Daisy

This plant is a daisy. The blossom is white and yellow. Name all of its parts.

Activity to Do

What is your favorite plant?

- Draw a picture of it.
- Color it.
- Label all of its parts.

Grammar and Writing

Time Order Words

We use words such as ***first, next, then, after, after that,*** and ***finally*** to tell the steps to do something or to tell the time order.

The Story of a Horse

First, the baby horse is born.

Next, he tries to stand.

Then the baby horse eats.

After that, he grows.

Finally, he is a big horse.

Practice

Write a time order word from the box to complete the sentence.

next then finally

1. First, there is an egg.
2. ________, it becomes a caterpillar.
3. ________, it makes a cocoon.
4. ________, it becomes a moth.

Apply

Talk about how watermelons grow.

Example: First, you can plant a seed.

Write

Draw a picture of a plant. How does it grow?

First, plant a seed and give it water. Then you wait to see green leaves. Finally, you will see a flower.

91–92

Reading 3
Prepare to Read

These words will help you understand the reading.

Vocabulary

Words to Know

1. Many animals live on our planet.

2. They all live together.

3. Birds eat seeds to grow.

4. Animals and plants are part of the food chain.

Sight Words

- many
- they
- all
- eat

Story Words

- animals
- birds
- food chain

Your Turn

Pick one word from either box.

Use the word in a sentence.

WB 93

Phonics

Long *i*

Look at each picture and word.

Listen to the letter sounds.

Say the word.

Your Turn

Name the pictures. Which words have the same sound as the ***i*** in ***ice***?

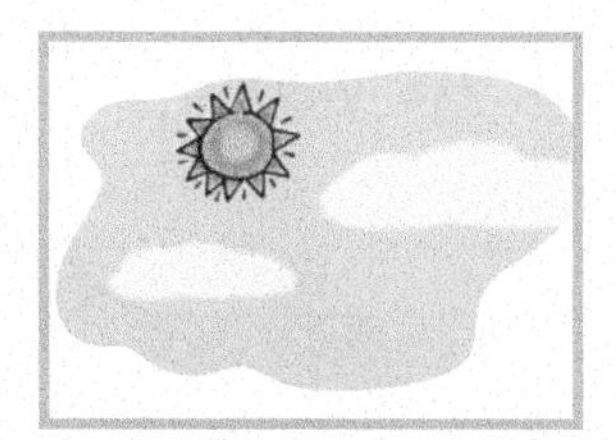

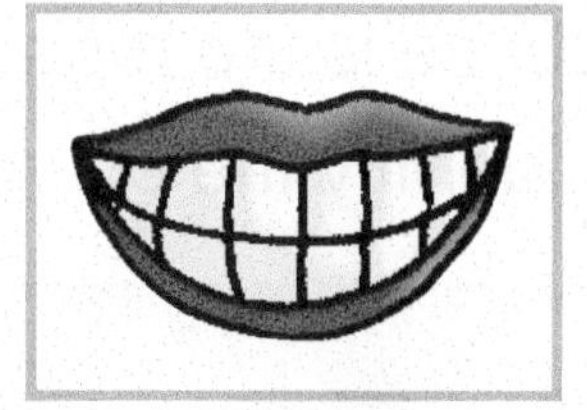

Story Preview

fish

bird

What is the story about?

trees

bats

fox

The story is about some animals that live on our planet.

Reading Strategy	Cause and Effect

The cause is the reason an effect happens. As you read, identify the causes and their effects.

Animals

On Your Own

by Anya Hansen
illustrated by
Nick Dimitriadis

Many kinds of animals live on Earth. They all need food and water. This lake is where some fish live. Most fish eat plants in the water.

Many bats live in caves. At night, the bats fly out of the cave to look for food. Most bats eat bugs.

All birds must eat. They may eat bugs and seeds. This blue jay eats seeds from a plant. The seeds will help the blue jay grow.

When birds grow, they can fly! They look for food, like bugs. Most birds live in trees.

A gray fox can live in the woods. Foxes eat small animals, like birds. Foxes are part of the food chain.

Gray foxes can climb trees. Then they can look for food. The birds fly away because the fox climbs the tree.

All animals need food and water.
Fish live in the water. Fish can swim.
Most birds live in trees. A gray fox
climbs trees to find food. There are
many kinds of animals on planet Earth.

Think It Over

**Read the questions. Say the answers.
Use Sight Words and Story Words.**

1. What animals did you meet in the story?
2. How do gray foxes find food?
3. What might cause a bird to fly away from the trees?
4. What do you need to live?

Reading Strategy | **Cause and Effect**

How does understanding cause and effect help you read better?

95–96

Grammar and Writing

Nouns: Singular and Plural

Singular nouns name one person, place, or thing. Plural nouns name more than one. Add ***-s*** or ***-es*** to make a noun plural.

a bat   two bat**s**   two fox**es**

Use ***an*** before singular nouns that start with ***a, e, i, o, u***.

an eagle

We can ask questions with ***How many . . .***

How many dogs are there? There is one **dog**. There are two **dogs**.

Practice A

Should the noun be singular or plural? Write the correct one.

1. There is one ______________. (frog/frogs)

2. There are two ______________. (rabbit/rabbits)

3. There is one ______________. (tiger/tigers)

Practice B

Write *a* or *an* on the line.

1. I see ____a____ lizard in the grass.
2. Do you see ________ ant on the ground?
3. She has ________ horse.
4. ________ duck is swimming in the pond.
5. ________ elephant has a trunk.

Apply

Look at the pictures in the story. With a partner, take turns asking and answering the question: How many ______ are on page ______?

Example: How many birds are on page 48?
There are 5 birds.

Write

Draw a picture of an animal you like. Write about it.

An owl is a bird. It lives in trees. An owl sleeps in the day. It hunts at night.

97–98

Put It All Together

Projects

Your teacher will help you choose one of these projects.

THE BIG QUESTION

How can living things help each other? Talk about it.

Written 

Write about a plant or an animal.

What does it look like? What do you like most about it? How does it help other things?

Oral

Introduce your favorite plant or animal.

Tell the class about your favorite plant or animal. Why do you like it so much?

Visual/Active

Be your favorite plant or animal.

Work with a partner. Move and make sounds like an animal, or move like a plant on a windy day.

99–100

Listening and Speaking Workshop

Explain How to Do Something

GO 4

Act out a chore and explain how to do it.

1 Prepare

Think of a chore you do at home. Use a chart like this one to list the steps.

HOW TO PLANT A SEED

1. Before you plant a seed, fill a flowerpot with soil.

↓

2. Then make a small hole in the soil for the seed.

↓

3. Put one seed in the hole. Cover the seed with soil.

↓

4. Water the soil and put the flowerpot in a sunny place.

Useful Language

Listen and repeat.

- I'll explain how to . . .
- First, you . . .
- Like this. (showing pic)
- What's next?
- Then you . . .
- After that, you . . .
- Finally, you . . .

Choose pictures to use in your presentation.
Draw a poster or bring props to class.

② Practice and Present

Practice with a partner. Use your chart and props. Then act out the steps for your class. Explain how to do the chore. Answer people's questions.

As you speak, do this:

- Use words such as *before, then, after, first, next, after that,* and *finally.*
- Speak slowly and in complete sentences.

As you listen, do this:

- Listen for what you already know.
- Look at the visuals or props.
- Take notes or draw pictures.

③ Evaluate

- Did you listen for things you already knew?
- Did you understand the directions for each chore?

More Practice

Think of a chore many people don't know how to do. Explain how to do it. Ask a partner to give the chore a title, such as "How to ________," summarize the most important thing, and explain a few steps.

Writing Workshop

Write an Expository Paragraph

Expository writing means explaining something by using facts and details.

1. **Prewrite** Think of an animal you like. Draw a web. Write facts about the animal in the web.

Saba wrote about a horse in her web.

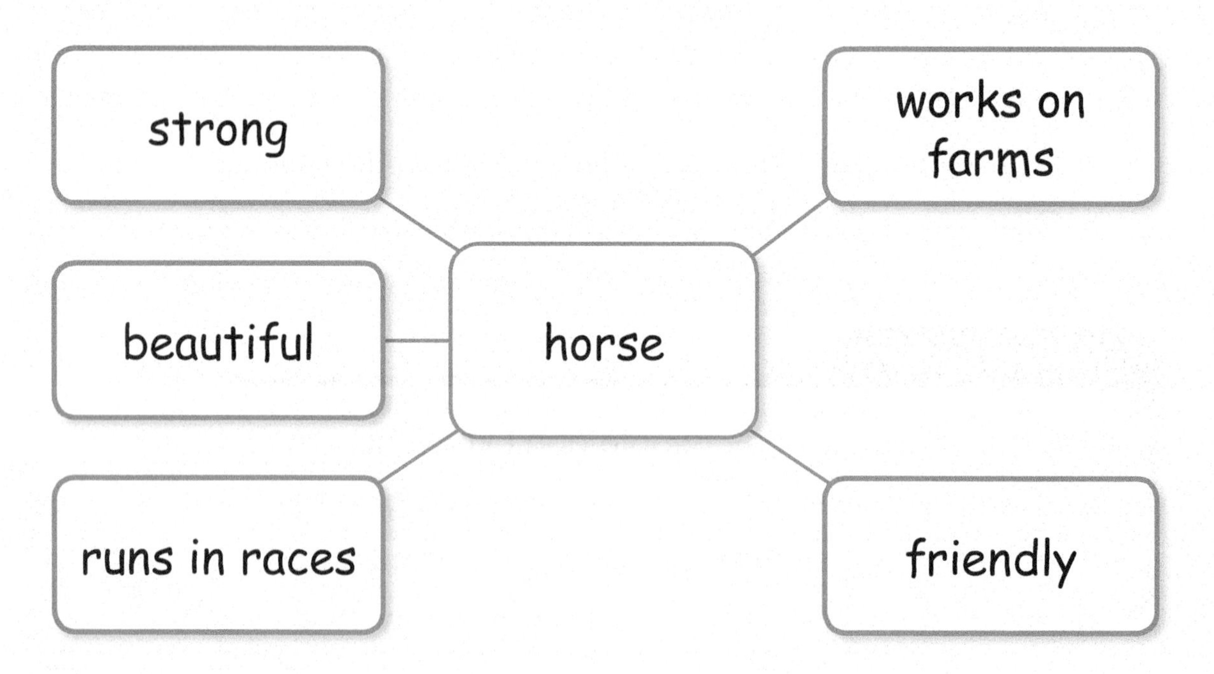

2 **Draft** Write an expository paragraph. Use new words from the unit. Use the ideas in your chart.

3 **Revise** Read your paragraph. Use the Revising Checklist to correct errors.

Revising Checklist

- ✔ Do I tell facts about the animal?
- ✔ Are all the sentences about the animal?

Writing Tip

To make your writing clear, give facts and details about the subject.

Here is Saba's paragraph.

My favorite animal is the horse. They are beautiful and very strong. Some horses work on farms. ~~there~~ There are also horses that run in races. My aunt has a ~~horses~~ horse. It's a work horse. So it doesn't race. It's friendly, so I can pet it.

④ **Edit** Trade papers. Correct your partner's paragraph. Use the Editing Checklist.

⑤ **Publish** Make a clean copy of your paragraph. Share it with the class.

Editing Checklist

- ✔ Pronouns and verbs agree.
- ✔ Verb tenses are correct.
- ✔ Sentences have different lengths, patterns, and connecting words (and).

WB 101–102

Fluency

For Each Reading...

1. Listen to the sentences.
2. Listen and use your finger to follow the words.
3. Listen, use your finger, and say the words.

Ducks can swim. Ducks kick their big, flat feet to swim.

Little Duck

Seeds make plants. A seed needs a lot of rain and a lot of sun.

Plants

Fish, bats, birds, and foxes live on our planet. All animals need food and water.

Animals

103–104

Unit 5

One World

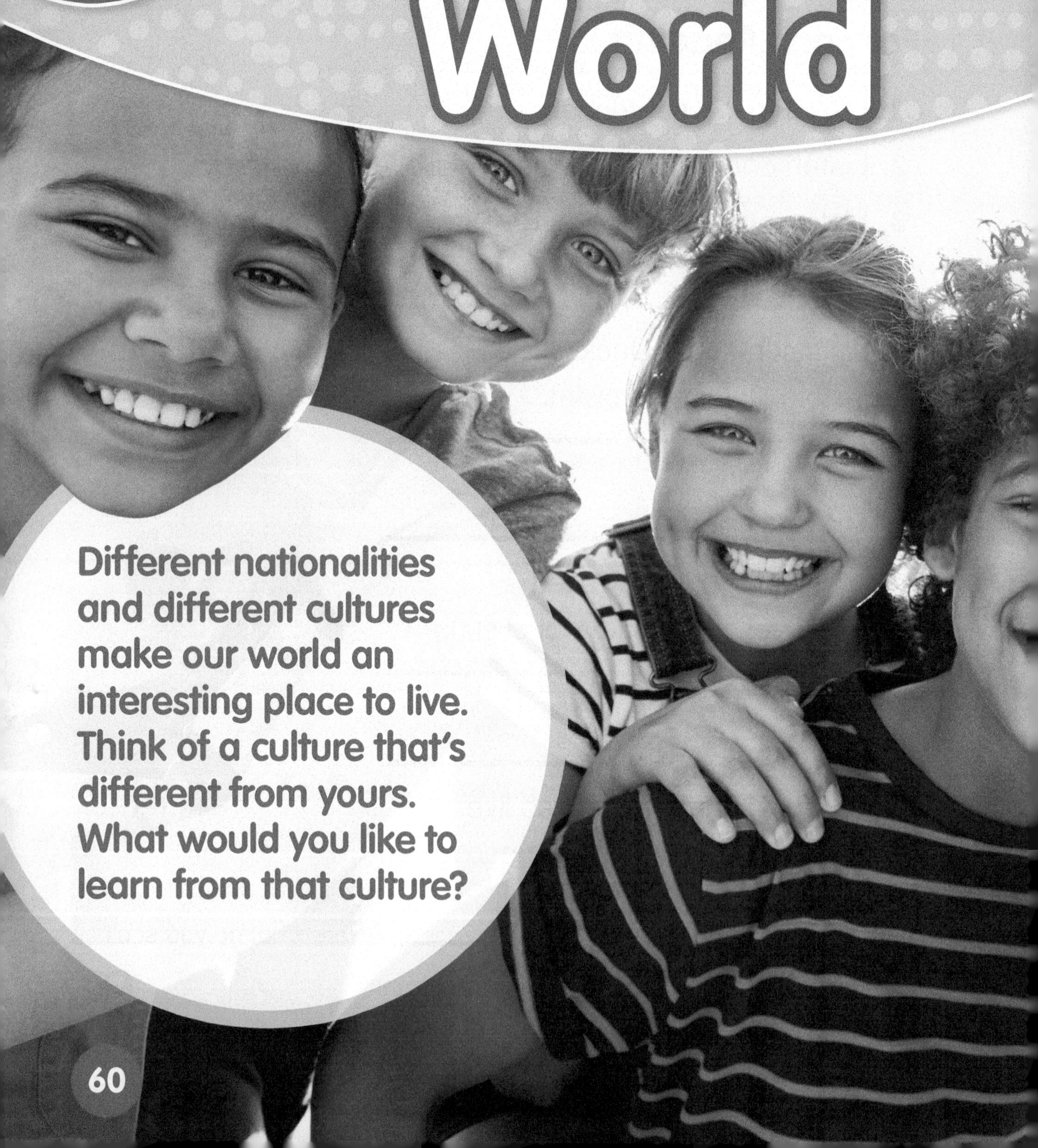

Different nationalities and different cultures make our world an interesting place to live. Think of a culture that's different from yours. What would you like to learn from that culture?

THE BIG QUESTION

What do you like most about living in your country?

View and Respond

Watch the video. What is it about?

Talk about the poster. What do you see?

Visit Pearson English Portal.

Build Unit Background

Many Nationalities, Different Cultures, One World!

Use what you know.

Different nationalities live in different countries around the world.

Colombians live in South America. They speak Spanish. Delicious food, such as empanadas, comes from South America.

Canada is in North America. Canada has two languages: English and French. It is famous for maple syrup.

These dolls can be seen all around Russia.

Kettle drums are a popular musical instrument in Jamaica.

Japan is in Asia. It is a beautiful country. People around the world love to eat sushi, a Japanese food.

Your Turn

What kind of food from your country is popular around the world? Tell the class about it.

Build Unit Background

Sing about One World

We Are All Citizens of the World

It is good; it is good;
it is good in our world.
We laugh, we learn,
and we live in harmony.
This world is for you and me.

It is good; it is good;

it is good in our world.

We share, we play,

and we live with peace and love.

I love our world.

Reading 1
Prepare to Read

These words will help you understand the reading.

Sight Words

one
two
wants
from

Story Words

bought
soccer
ball

Vocabulary

Words to Know

1. I have one head and two hands.

2. This boy wants you to know he is from Pakistan.

3. My mom bought me this soccer ball.

Your Turn

Pick one word from either box.

Use the word in a sentence.

Work with a partner.

107

Phonics

Long *o*

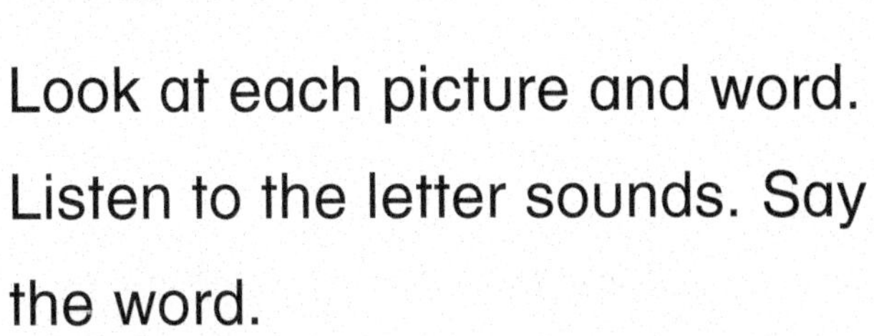

Look at each picture and word. Listen to the letter sounds. Say the word.

float

soap

toe

blow

108

Your Turn

Which letters stand for the sound in the middle of the word?

oa ay

ai ow

oa ie

ee oa

Story Preview

Reading Tip

Read on your own or with a small group.

Who is in the story?

Blake

Cliff

Joan

Joe

What is the story about?

football

soccer

Reading Strategy | **Make Inferences**

Sometimes a story does not tell you everything. Use what you know and story clues to get your own ideas. As you read, make inferences about the story.

Reading 1

One, Two, Three, Play!

On Your Own

by Ben Akin
illustrated by Mark Stephens

Blake just bought a football. He wants to play with Cliff and Joan. Blake likes to play in a football game.

Blake can throw and pass. Joan can run fast. Cliff can kick the football. Blake needs one more kid. Then they can play a game.

Can Joe play with Blake and Cliff and Joan? Joe is from another land. Joe has not seen a ball like this. Joe says, "This is not the same as in my land."

Joe shows Blake, Cliff, and Joan
his ball. Blake, Cliff, and Joan tell Joe
that it is a soccer ball. Joe says it is
named a football in his land. Joe says
he likes to play football in his land.

Blake tells Joe that this is
named a soccer ball in his land.
Blake tells Joe that soccer is fun
but football is fun, too. Blake
will teach Joe to play football.

Blake can pass to Joe. One, two, three, the football goes high. Can Joe get the football from Blake? Blake will teach Joe to catch and pass.

Joan shows Joe how to block
and run to the goal line. One,
two, three, Joe runs to the goal
line fast. He likes this game.
It is fun.

Cliff wants to play soccer. He wants to kick and run and score. Can Cliff play soccer? Joe can show Cliff how to play. Joe can coach Cliff.

Joe can use his feet to play soccer. Joe is fast on his feet. He can kick the soccer ball and score!

Think It Over

Read the questions. Say the answers.
Use Sight Words and Story Words.

1. What game does Blake like to play?
2. What else does Blake need to play football?
3. Who comes from another country?
4. Why is it good to learn to play and be friends with children from other cultures?

Reading Strategy	Make Inferences
How did making inferences help you understand the story?	

109–110

Grammar and Writing

Nouns: Proper and Common Nouns

Nouns name people, places, animals, and things. A proper noun names a specific person or place and always starts with a capital letter. **Stefan** and **Trinity Park** are proper nouns.

Common nouns are not actual or specific names. Examples: **pal** and **puppy** are common nouns.

My name is **Stefan**. I am from **Mexico**.

My friend **Felix** lives in **Madrid**.

Common Nouns	Proper Nouns
girl	Rosie
park	Trinity Park
city	Singapore

This is **Ava** with her puppy **Bo**.

Practice A

Capitalize the proper nouns in each sentence.

1. cancun is a city in mexico.
2. My friend juan traveled from mexico to argentina.
3. Is australia a country or a continent?

Practice B

Underline the common nouns in the sentences from Practice A.

Apply

Example: A: What is your best friend's name?

B: Her name is Mei.

Where does your best friend live?
Where do you live?

Write

Tell a story you know. Draw a picture of it.

My friend José can play the guitar. My dog Lola jumps when José plays music. Lola likes music!

111–112

Vocabulary

These words will help you understand the reading.

Words to Know

1. Yo-Yo Ma is one of the best cello players in the world.

2. The cello was too big for him.

3. He wanted to know how to play the cello.

4. His family went to live in the United States.

Sight Words

best
know
live
big

Story Words

cello
world
play

Your Turn

Pick one word from either box.

Use the word in a sentence.

113

Phonics

Wh; Vowel Diphthongs

Look at each picture and word.

Listen to the letter sounds.

Say the word.

brown **outside**

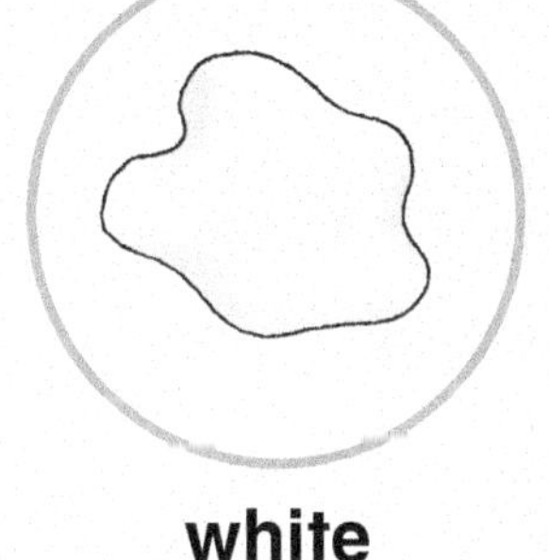

white

Your Turn

Sound out the words. Point to the word for the picture. Write the word.

own owl

shout sheet

moose mouth

wheel whale

Story Preview

Reading Tip

To help you understand the story, make pictures in your mind about the people, places, and events in the story.

Who is in the story?

Yo-Yo Ma

His family

Where does the story happen?

France

U.S.

Reading Strategy | **Visualizing**

Visualizing, or picturing the story in your mind as you read, will help you understand and enjoy the story.

Yo-Yo Ma

On Your Own

by Anya Hansen

Yo-Yo Ma plays music. He plays the cello. He is one of the best cello players in the world.

Yo-Yo Ma's mom and dad were from China. When he was born, they were in France. Yo-Yo grew up in France.

Yo-Yo Ma's mom and dad played music. His sister also played music. Yo-Yo wanted to play music, too. He wanted to know how to play the cello.

The cello is big. But Yo-Yo Ma was a small boy. One day, his dad made a cello for him. It was still too big. Yo-Yo had to sit on big books to play his cello!

Yo-Yo Ma was very good at the cello, but he still worked hard. He wanted to be better at playing the cello.

Yo-Yo Ma's family went to a new land. They went to live in America. His dad wanted Yo-Yo to learn more about the cello. Many people came to hear Yo-Yo play. He wrote new music, too.

Today Yo-Yo Ma is one of the best cello players in the world. He also has two children. He and his family live in America.

Think It Over

Read the questions. Say the answers.
Use Sight Words and Story Words.

1. Who is Yo-Yo Ma?
2. What did Yo-Yo want to do as a boy?
3. How did Yo-Yo's dad help him?
4. What two things do you think helped Yo-Yo Ma become successful?

Reading Strategy	Visualizing

How did picturing the story in your mind help you understand and enjoy it?

115–116

Grammar and Writing

Simple Past of *Be*: *Was* and *Were*

Use ***was*** with *I, he, she,* and *it.*

I **was** in Singapore last month. He/She **was** in Singapore last month.

Use ***were*** with *you, we,* and *they.*

We/They/You **were** in Singapore last month.

To make a negative statement, use ***was not*** or ***were not***.

It **wasn't** there a few minutes ago. You **were not** in Singapore last month.

was not → **wasn't**
were not → **weren't**

To make *Yes/No* questions, use ***was*** or ***were***.

Was she in Singapore last month?	Yes, she **was**.
Were you in Singapore last month?	No, I **wasn't**.
Were they in Singapore last month?	Yes, they **were**.

To make questions with ***where***, begin the question with *Where* + ***was*** or ***were***.

Where were you last month? We **were** in Singapore.

Practice A

Use *was* or *were* to complete the sentences.

1. My cat ___was___ at the vet yesterday.
2. It ______________ sick.
3. We ______________ worried.
4. My parents ______________ glad to go home.

Practice B

Write two negative sentences about Yo-Yo Ma (Reading 2) in your notebook. Use the simple past of *be*.

Apply

Example: A: Were you home yesterday?

B: No, I wasn't.

Was your family at home yesterday?

Where were they?

Write

Write a journal entry. Draw a picture.

Last week, my cousins were at our house. My mom cooked delicious food. We were sad when they left.

117–118

Vocabulary

These words will help you understand the reading.

Words to Know

1. This chef worked in a kitchen, where he made food.

2. The chef helped make dinner tonight. He will do it again tomorrow night.

3. The crew likes working on a cruise ship.

Sight Words

where
worked
again

Story Words

chef
cruise
crew

Your Turn

Pick one word from either box.

Use the word in a sentence.

119

Phonics

Letters: *ue, ui, ew*

Look at each picture and word.

Listen to the letter sounds.

Say the word.

glue

new

fruit

WB 120

Your Turn

Name the pictures. Which words have the same sound as the *ue* in ***glue***?

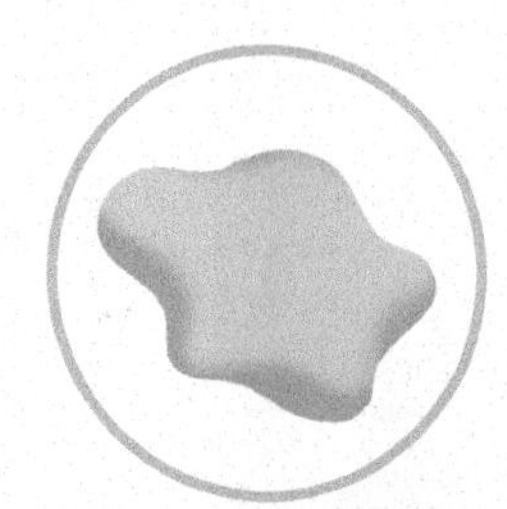

Story Preview

Who is in the story?

chef

crew

Where does the story happen?

cruise ship

Reading Strategy | **Compare and Contrast**

Compare things to see how they are the same. Contrast things to see how they are different. As you read, see how things are alike and different.

Life on a Cruise Ship

On Your Own

Reading 3

Mario is a chef on a cruise ship. A cruise ship is like a big hotel on the water. This ship is going from Spain to Italy. Some cruise ships hold thousands of passengers.

Lots of people work on this ship. They come from all over the world. A large cruise ship might have 300 crew members just in the kitchen.

The passengers on the ship also come from all over the world. Not everyone likes the same kind of food. So Mario's staff cooks foods from all over the world. They cook meals for the crew, too.

Mario works very hard. He plans the menus long before the ship sails. Then he buys the food. Some of the food will be frozen. But some of it will be fresh. Bakers on the ship make fresh breads and desserts.

Some passengers eat in the main dining room. There are also other places to eat on a cruise ship. You can find a place to eat pizza or pasta. You can find a place to eat barbeque. You can even find a place to eat sushi. And Mario and his crew are in charge of it all!

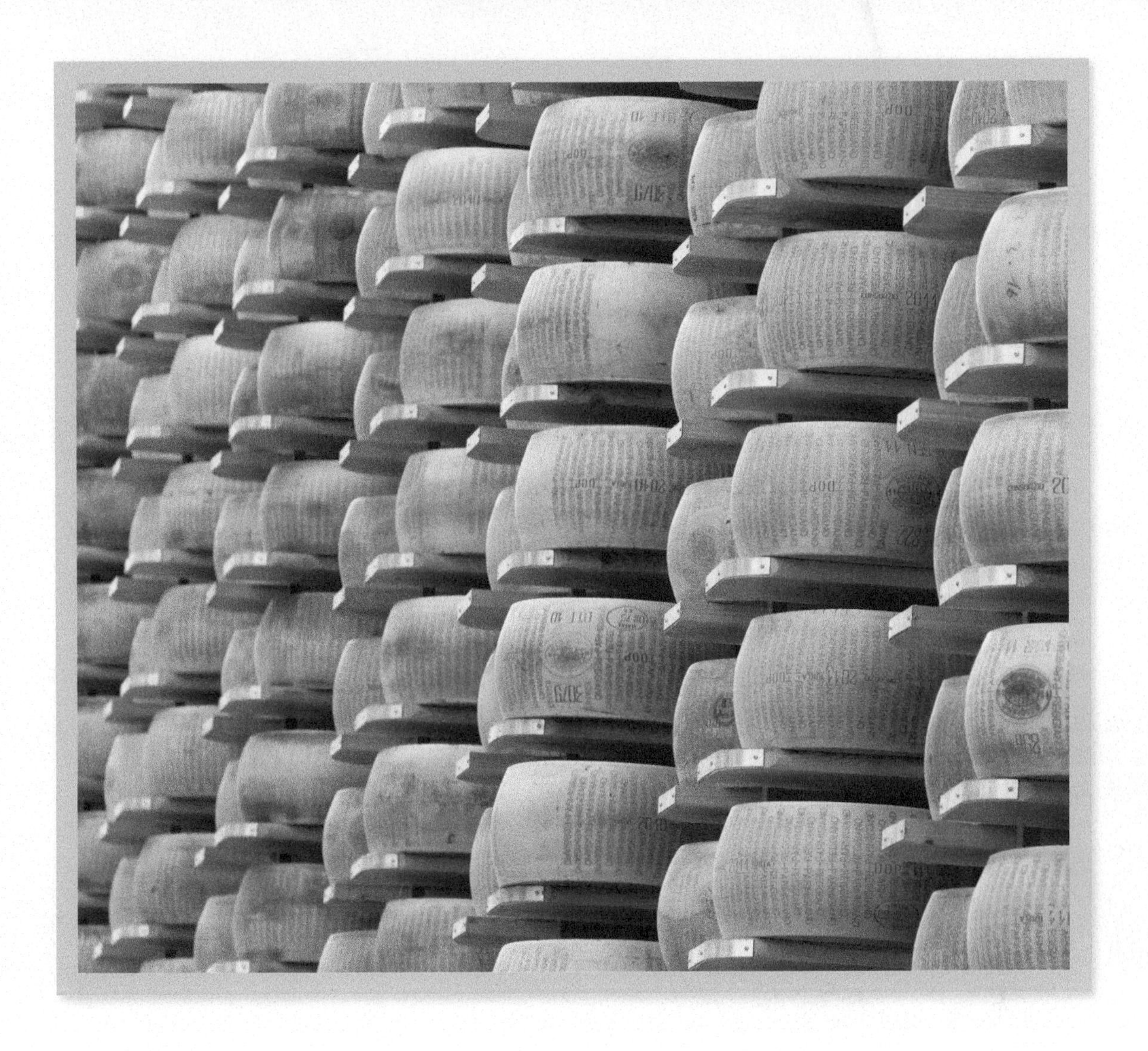

Cruise ships make many stops along the way. At each stop, Mario buys fresh food from the people who live there. He might buy cheese from Italy. He might buy fruit from Hawaii. What he buys depends on where the ship is sailing.

When the cruise is over, the passengers return home. Mario and his crew get some rest. They have worked very hard. But when it's time for the next cruise, they'll do it all over again!

Think It Over

Read the questions. Say the answers.
Use Sight Words and Story Words.

1. What is this story about?
2. What is a cruise chef's job?
3. Who helps a cruise chef do his or her job?
4. How is a cruise chef's job like a chef's job in a restaurant on land? How is it different?

Reading Strategy | **Compare and Contrast**

How did comparing and contrasting help you understand the story?

121–122

A CLOSER LOOK AT...

A Cruise Ship

Most cruise ships have a big play area.
There are lots of fun things for children to do!

A chef wears a special uniform. Chefs everywhere have similar uniforms.

Activitiy to Do

Draw a chef on a cruise ship.

- Color it.
- Show your picture.
- Tell your own story about the chef.

Grammar and Writing

The Simple Past

To form the simple past of most regular verbs, add ***-ed*** to the verb.

It **rained** yesterday. We **stayed** home and **played** games.

Irregular verbs have a different simple past form:

Base form		Past tense
eat	→	**ate**
come	→	**came**

Base form		Past tense
have	→	**had**
leave	→	**left**

Base form		Past tense
see	→	**saw**
go	→	**went**

We **had** fun at home last night.

To make negative statements in the simple past, use ***did not***.

They **did not see** their friends yesterday. He **did not see** you yesterday.

did not → **didn't**

To ask questions with **when**, begin with ***When*** + ***did***.

When did it rain? It **rained** last night.

Practice A

Change these sentences into the simple past.
Write them in your notebook.

1. Li uses the computer.
2. Ana plays with her cat.
3. We do our homework.

Practice B

Change the sentences in Practice A into negative sentences. Write them in your notebook.

Li **did not use** the computer.

Apply

Example: A: When did you call me?

B: I called you yesterday.

walk your dog
see a movie
read a book

Write

What did you do yesterday? Draw a picture and write.

Yesterday, Joe and I played at the playground. Then we ate snacks.

123–124

Put It All Together

Projects

Your teacher will help you choose one of these projects.

Written 

Write about your country.

Why is your country a good place to live? Write about it.

THE BIG QUESTION

What do you like most about living in your country? Talk about it.

Oral

Say hello in another language.

Do you know how people in other cultures say “hello”? Say “hello” in another language. Use gestures and words.

Visual/Active

Can you act out a story?

Have you visited a new city or another country? What was it like living in another place? Tell your classmates about it. Use gestures to make your story interesting.

125–126

Listening and Speaking Workshop

A Skit

GO 10

Act out a skit. Tell a story about a problem you solved for a friend.

Useful Language

Listen and repeat.

- Are you ok?
- What's the problem?
- Can I help you? / I can help you.
- Let's . . .

1 Prepare

Think of a problem you solved for a friend. Tell this story to a partner. Then listen to your partner's story. Choose one story. Use a chart like this to plan a skit with your partner.

Who?	When and Where?
Matt and me	Saturday morning in the park
Problem	**Solution**
Matt had a soccer ball. He didn't know how to play soccer and wanted to learn.	I know how to play soccer so I taught Matt.

Decide what props to use for the skit. Find them in the class or bring them from home.

② Practice and Present

Practice the skit with a partner. The skit should tell a story. Listen to your partner to know when to speak and move. Then act out your skit for the class.

As you speak, do this:

- Speak the way you talk to your friends.
- Use your voice and body to show feelings.

As you listen, do this:

- Look at the actors to help you listen and understand.
- Use what you know to help you understand.
- If something isn't clear, listen for clues and think again.

③ Evaluate

- Did your skit tell a story?
- Did you speak the way you talk to your friends?
- Did you understand what people said?

More Practice

Plan and practice a skit with a partner to show how to solve a problem. Present it to two kids. Ask them to:

- Give the skit a title.
- Summarize the main points and details of the skit.

Writing Workshop

Write a Narrative

A narrative is a story. Most narratives use verbs in the past tense. All the sentences in the narrative help tell the story.

> Last year, we moved to a new house. The people next door had a big bird. At first, I was scared. Then one day we met them. I talked to the bird. She made lots of noise. Her name was Belle. That means beautiful. She is a nice bird. I love Belle.

Writing Tip

Always review and edit your writing, or have someone edit it for you. Check for spelling mistakes.

① **Prewrite** Think of a funny story that happened to you. Draw a story map and write in it.

Marco wrote a story map.

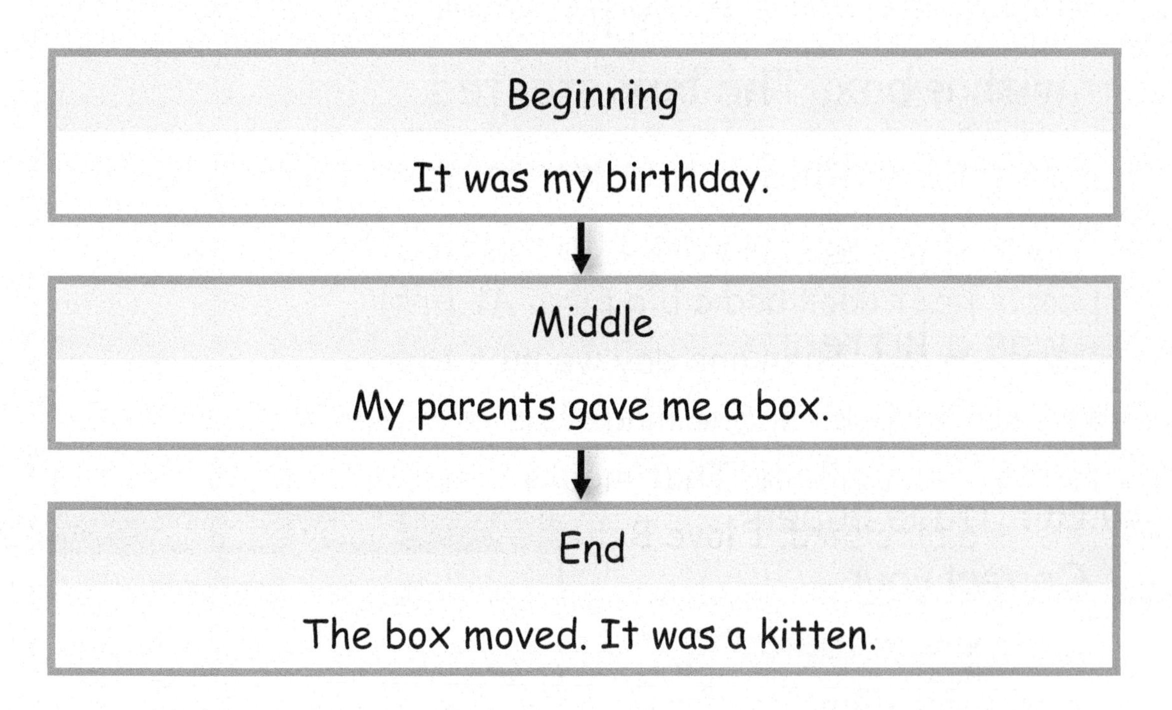

② **Draft** Write a narrative. Use new words from the unit. Use the ideas in your chart.

③ **Revise** Read your paragraph. Use the Revising Checklist to correct errors.

Revising Checklist

✔ Did all the sentences help tell my story?

✔ Were verbs in the past?

Here is Marco's narrative.

It was my birthday and my mom and dad ~~come~~ came home with a box. The box started to roll around. Then my mom and dad ~~open~~ opened the box. Inside was a kitten!

4 **Edit** Trade papers. Correct your partner's paragraph. Use the Editing Checklist.

5 **Publish** Make a clean copy of your paragraph. Share it.

Editing Checklist

- ✔ Subjects and verbs agree.
- ✔ Verb tenses are correct.
- ✔ There are different sentence lengths and patterns, and connecting words (*and*).

WB 127–128

Fluency

For Each Reading...

1. Listen to the sentences. Use your finger to follow the words.
2. Read aloud for one minute. Count the number of words you read.

One, Two, Three, Play! is a story about football	9
and soccer. Cliff wants to play soccer. He wants	18
to kick and run and score. Joe can show Cliff	28
how to play. Joe is fast on his feet. He is good!	40

3. Now read for your teacher.

129–130

Unit 6

Friendships

It is nice to have friends! Friends are important in our lives. Tell the class about what you like to do with your friends.

What makes a good friend?

View and Respond

Watch the video. What is it about?

Talk about the poster. What do you see?

Visit Pearson English Portal.

Build Unit Background

What Do You Know about Friendships?

Use what you know.

A friend plays with you.

A friend helps you.

A friend cares
for you.

A friend loves you.

Your Turn

Who is your best
friend? Why is your
friend special? Tell
the class about it.

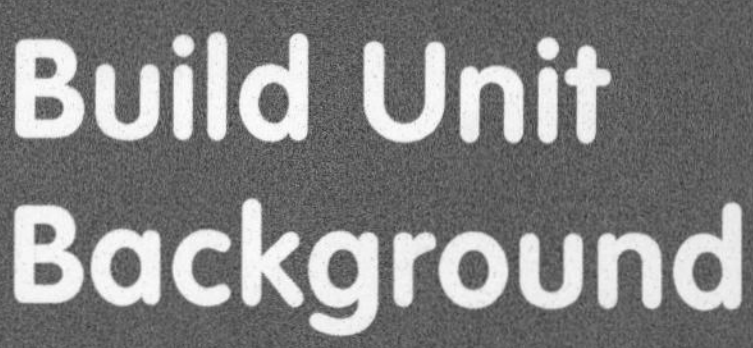

Build Unit Background

Sing about Friendships

My Friend, Your Friend

I'm your friend and you are my friend,
each and every day.
I'm your friend and you are my friend.
We sing songs and play fun games.

In our school or in our backyard,

we're as happy as can be.

I'm your friend and you are my friend.

I love you and you love me!

Vocabulary

These words will help you understand the reading.

Words to Know

1. Let's all get together.

2. The door is open. Please come in!

Sight Words

together
open
come

Story Words

friends
music

3. Susan and I are friends. We like music.

Your Turn

Pick one word from either box.

Use the word in a sentence.

Work with a partner.

133

Phonics

Letters: *oo*

Phonics

moon

book

Look at each picture and word. Listen to the letter sounds. Say the word.

134

Your Turn

Sound out the words. Point to the word for the picture. Write the word.

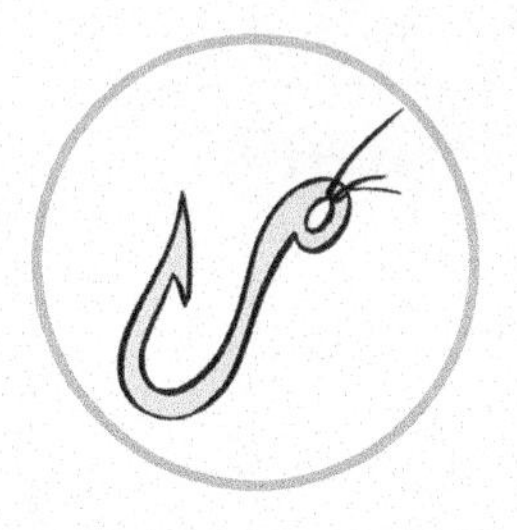

hook **hack**

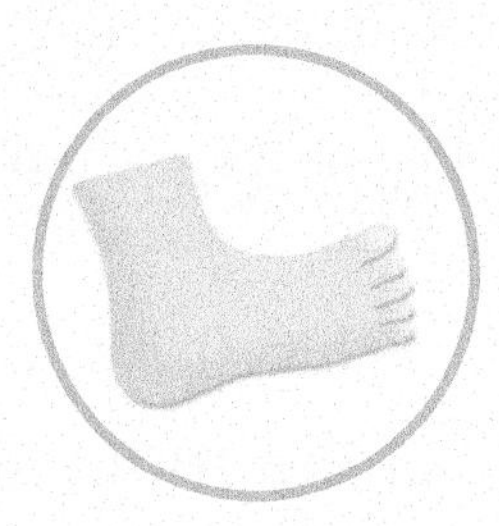

fat **foot**

school **scale**

ruff **roof**

Story Preview

Reading Tip

When you read, look for the important ideas.

Who is in the story?

Max

Ray

Where does the story happen?

school

Reading Strategy **Main Idea and Details**

The main idea is what a story is about. The details give more information about the main idea. As you read, look for the main idea.

Max and Ray

Reading 1

On Your Own

by Scott Carl
illustrated by Anne Kennedy

Meet Max and Ray. Max and Ray are best friends. Max and Ray have a lot of fun in school together.

Max and Ray come together to fix a big box. The box is open on top. It has red, blue, and striped balls. Max and Ray will tape its side and fix it up.

Max likes math best. He is good
at adding. Max can help Ray count
and add in his math book.

Ray likes spelling best. Ray can spell and print well. He is good at spelling big words. Ray can help Max spell *frog* and *cat* and *jump*.

Max and Ray play cool music together. Max toots his sax while Ray claps and sings.

Come on! Tap your foot and
shake your head. Hear the
cool tunes of Max and Ray.

Max and Ray have fun at school and fun at play. Max and Ray have fun all day!

Think It Over

Read the questions. Say the answers.
Use Sight Words and Story Words.

1. Who are Max and Ray?
2. What is Max good at? What is Ray good at?
3. How do Max and Ray help each other?
4. What do Max and Ray do for fun?
5. Why are friends important?

Reading Strategy | **Main Ideas and Details**

Use the main ideas and details to summarize the story.

135–136

Grammar and Writing

Imperatives

We use imperatives to give commands, give directions, or tell someone how to do something.

To make an imperative, use the base form of the verb.

To make a negative imperative, use ***Do*** + ***not***.

Cookie Recipe

First, **put** flour, sugar, water, and oil in a bowl.

Next, **add** eggs and **mix** it all in the bowl.

Then **roll** the cookie dough.

Finally, **bake** the cookies, but **do not burn** them!

Practice A

Underline the imperative in each sentence.

1. First, get on the bicycle.
2. Now, put your feet on the pedals.
3. Push down on the pedals.
4. To stop, squeeze the hand brakes.

Practice B

Change these sentences into imperatives. Write the sentences in your notebook.

1. You will turn right at the corner.
2. You should copy these words in your notebook.
3. You should close your books.
4. You should do your homework.

Apply

Take turns. Say commands. Guess the action.

Example: A: Dribble and shoot the ball.

B: You're playing basketball!

bake a cake play soccer walk a dog

Write

Tell how to make something. Draw the steps.

How to Make a Sand Castle

Fill a bucket with sand. Turn the bucket upside down. Pat the top to loosen the sand. Make rectangles for doors. Make a path to your castle.

137–138

Vocabulary

These words will help you understand the reading.

Sight Words

over
baby
different

Story Words

hippopotamus
tortoise

Words to Know

1. Look over the babies carefully. Each baby is different.

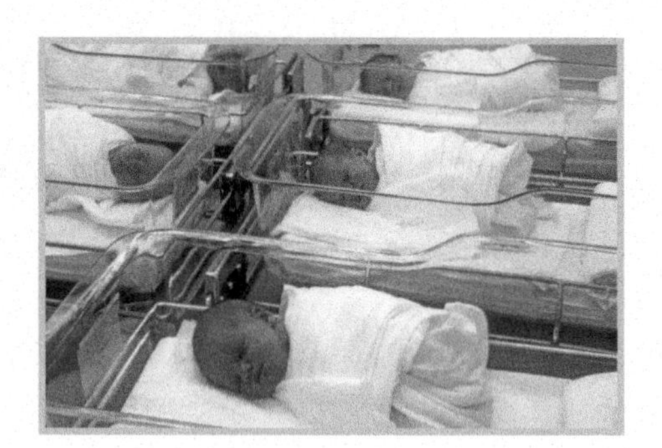

2. A hippopotamus is a big animal.

3. A tortoise carries its own house!

Your Turn

Pick one word from either box.

Use the word in a sentence.

139

Phonics

R-controlled vowels: *ir, ur, er*

Look at each picture and word.

Listen to the letter sounds.

Say the word.

Your Turn

Name the pictures. Which words have the same sound you hear in ***fern***?

Story Preview

Who is in the story?

tortoise

hippopotamus

What is this story about?

The story is about two friends.

Reading Strategy | **Summarize**

To summarize is to choose only the important information in the story. As you read, look for the most important information in the story.

Reading 2

Owen and Mzee

On Your Own

by Morgan Joyce

Meet Owen and Mzee.
They are different, but
they are a family.

Owen is a hippopotamus that has lost his herd. Owen likes to stay close to Mzee. He may think Mzee is like his dad.

Mzee is green and brown and has a hard shell. Look at him stick his neck out of his shell.

Mzee is 120 years old! A tortoise has a very long life.

Owen is a baby hippopotamus,
and he is just one year old!

A hippopotamus plays in dirt and
grass. A mom or dad must help keep
him safe because he is a baby.

Owen is still small for a hippopotamus. Can you see him in this big grass?

Can you see this little hippopotamus play in big, tall grass?

Mzee will watch over Owen and keep him safe. Owen will not be sad and will not get hurt.
This hippopotamus and this tortoise are a good family because they stay together day and night.

Think It Over

Read the questions. Say the answers.
Use Sight Words and Story Words.

1. Who are Owen and Mzee?
2. Why does Owen need a dad?
3. Why are Owen and Mzee a good family?
4. What do you think makes a good family?

Reading Strategy	Summarize
Use the important information that you found to summarize Owen and Mzee's story.	

141–142

A CLOSER LOOK AT...

Tortoises

Giant tortoise

Tortoises are related to turtles. They live on land. A hard shell protects a tortoise. Tortoises hide in their shells.

This baby tortoise is called a hatchling. It weighed only about 3 pounds at birth. It will stay with its mother until it can take care of itself.

Activity to Do

Draw a tortoise.

- Label its head.
- Label its feet.
- Label its shell.

Then color your tortoise.

Grammar and Writing

And/Or

Use ***and*** to show *plus*. Use ***and*** to connect two nouns, two verbs, or two adjectives.

Fong **and** Kwan are my friends.

Use ***or*** to show a choice.

Do you want milk **or** juice?

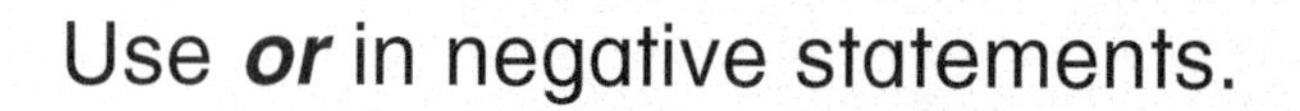

Use ***or*** in negative statements.

Sang Min does not like art **or** music. He likes math!

Practice A

Fill in the blanks with *and* or *or*.

1. I like soccer ___and___ table tennis.
2. Do you play the violin ______________ the piano?
3. Do you like apples ______________ oranges?
4. She likes music ______________ art.
5. Is this crayon red ______________ blue?

Practice B

Write a sentence and a question. Use these words in each.

1. dancing **and** acting
2. dancing **or** acting

Apply

Make sentences with the words in the box. Use *and* or *or*.

friendly	mean
happy	loud
polite	quiet

Example: A: *Sergio is not mean or loud.*

B: *I'm serious and smart.*

Write

Write about Owen and Mzee. Compare them.

Example:

Owen and Mzee are friends. Owen is a hippopotamus. He doesn't have a shell or webbed feet. Mzee is a tortoise. He is old and slow.

143–144

Vocabulary

These words will help you understand the reading.

Sight Words

work
enjoy
build
meet

Story Words

welcome
neighborhood
project

Words to Know

1. Kids like to play and work together.

2. My friend and I enjoy doing different things.

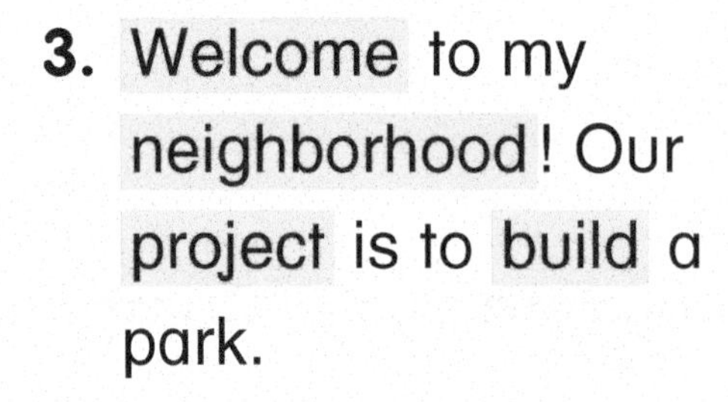

3. Welcome to my neighborhood! Our project is to build a park.

4. My friends and I meet at the fence.

Your Turn

Pick one word from either box.

Use the word in a sentence.

145

Phonics

R-controlled vowels: *ar*

Phonics

card

Look at each picture and word.

Listen to the letter sounds.

Say the word.

car

jar

park

Your Turn

146

Name the pictures. Which words have the same sound as the *ar* in ***card***? Write the words.

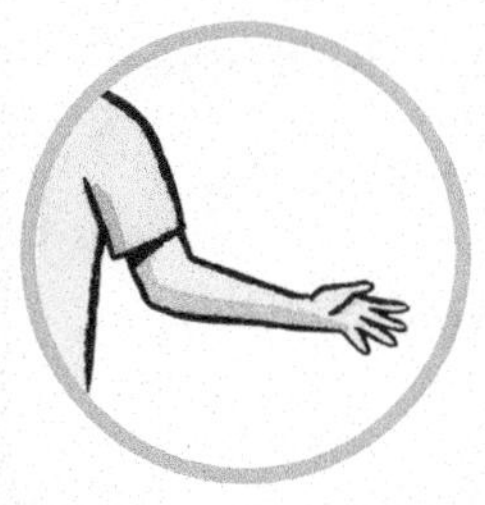

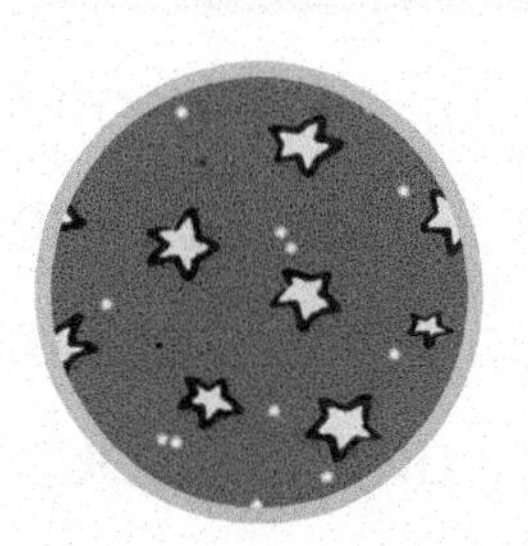

Story Preview

Reading Tip

Ask a partner a question about the story. Use Sight Words and Story Words.

Who is in this story?

City Mouse and Country Mouse

What is the story about?

The story is about a city mouse and a country mouse.

Reading Strategy | **Prior Knowledge**

Use your prior knowledge, or what you already know about a topic, to help you understand the story. As you read, think about what you already know about the city and the countryside.

City Mouse and Country Mouse

On Your Own

Reading 3

by Anya Hansen
illustrated by Dave Kirwan

Welcome! My name is City Mouse. I live in the city. This is a neighborhood in my city. My city has many buildings, people, and mice. The country is over that hill.

Mice from the city and the country meet to plan a project. We will work together to build a new park in my neighborhood. After we are done with our project, we will enjoy going to our new park.

Mice from the city and the country all help to work on the park. I make a new friend as I paint the fence. His name is Country Mouse. He is from the country and lives over the hill.

My new friend is different from me. In the country, he does not live in a neighborhood with lots of buildings. Country Mouse lives on a big farm. There are many other animals that live on the farm, like cows, horses, and ducks.

Take a look! After a lot of hard work, we finally finished our project. We built a new park! It is a fun place where friends can play together. Country Mouse and I will meet in the park when he visits my city.

Country Mouse and I play, eat, and talk in the park. We also ride our bikes, skate, and go for walks. At lunchtime, we eat cheese and corn on the cob from his farm. Country Mouse and I have a lot of fun together!

Our park has a big playground with a lot of fun toys. Country Mouse likes the swings next to the slide, and I play in the sandbox along the fence. We worked hard together to build our new park. We had a lot of fun, too!

Read the questions. Say the answers.
Use Sight Words and Story Words.

1. Where do the two mice live?
2. How is the city different from the countryside?
3. How do the mice become friends?
4. What do you know about working with others?

Speaking Tip

Read the story out loud, using facial expressions to make it more enjoyable.

Reading Strategy	Prior Knowledge

How did using prior knowledge help you understand the reading?

147–148

Grammar and Writing

Prepositions

Prepositions can tell us where something is. Some common prepositions are ***in***, ***inside***, ***on***, ***over***, ***through***, and ***under***.

Bats fly **in** the air.

Armadillos look **through** the grass for bugs.

Practice A

Write a preposition from the box to complete the sentence.

under	over	on

1. The mouse is ______________ the ground.

2. The cow eats grass ______________ the tree.

3. Look at the duck flying ______________ the water!

Practice B

Fill in the blanks with a preposition.

1. Mice crawl ___through___ tunnels.
2. Hawks fly ____________ the sky.
3. Lizards sit ____________ rocks.
4. Bats live ____________ caves.

Apply

Ask your partner to do something.
Use three words from the box.

Example: Sit in the chair!

over	under
desk	hop
walk	on
through	floor
door	

Write

Draw two animals. Compare and contrast them.

I like owls and mice.
Owls live in trees or in barns.
Mice live under the ground,
in fields, or in barns.

149–150

Put It All Together

Projects

Your teacher will help you choose one of these projects.

Written 

Write about a friend.

Who is your friend? When did you meet your friend? What do you do together? Write about it.

THE BIG QUESTION

What makes a good friend? Talk about it.

Talk about your friends.
Tell the class about your friends and what makes them special.

Visual/Active

Act out what you do with your friends.
Work with two classmates. Act out a favorite game or activity you like to do with friends.

WB 151–152

Listening and Speaking Workshop

An Interview 

Interview a classmate about what he or she likes to do.

① Prepare

Use a chart to plan your questions.

Useful Language	
What?	What do you like to do?
Where?	Where do you listen to music?
When?	When do you listen to music?
Who?	Who do you listen to music with?
Why?	Why do you listen to music?

② Practice and Present

Practice your interview with a partner. Use your chart and ask questions. Listen closely. Does your partner explain what he or she likes to do? Next, interview your partner in front of the class.

Useful Language

Listen and repeat the questions in the chart above.

As you speak, do this:

- Look at the person as you ask questions.
- Explain answers with details.
- Use complete sentences.

Speaking Tip

Speak in short and long sentences. To make long sentences, use words like *and*, *but*, or *because*.

As you listen, do this:

- Use what you know to help you understand.
- Listen for details and take notes.
- If you don't understand something, ask for help.

Listening Tip

Listen to your teacher. Learn the expression, *What's up?* How can you answer that question?

3 Evaluate

- How did what you know help you understand?
- Did you understand the other interviews?
- Retell what you learned in an interview.

Writing Workshop

Write to Compare and Contrast

Compare and contrast means to show how two things are alike or different.

My two best friends are Ana and Kate. They are the same in some ways. Ana and Kate are both smart and friendly. They are different, too. Ana is nine. She likes sports. Kate is seven and likes ballet.

1. **Prewrite** Think about two friends. Draw a Venn diagram. Write ideas in the chart. How are your friends alike or different?

   Miguel wrote in his Venn diagram.

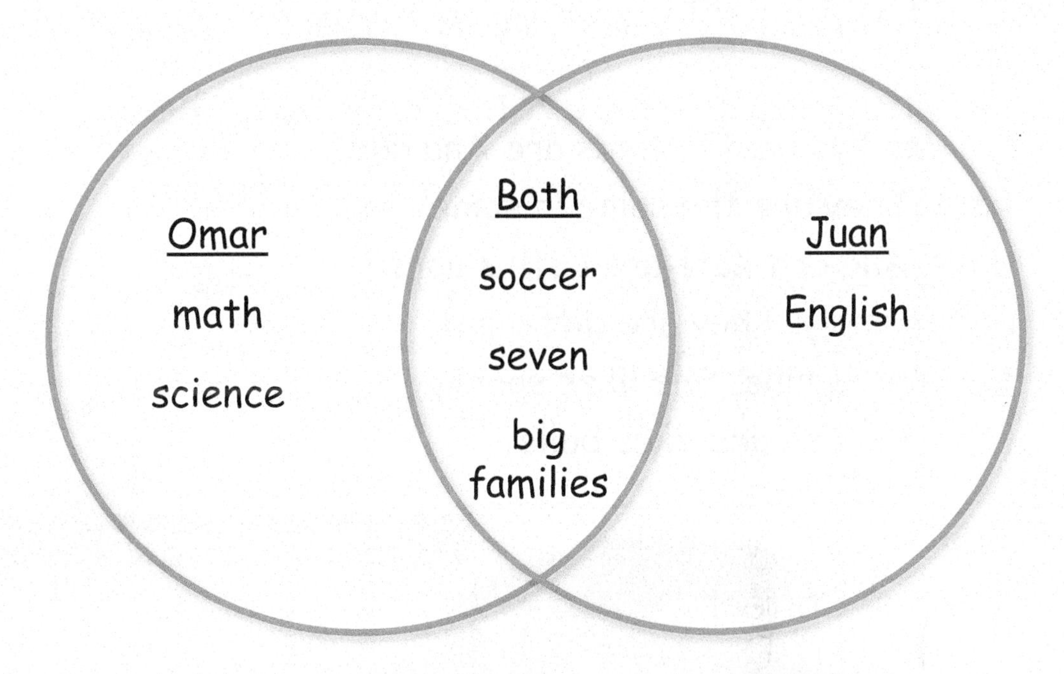

2. **Draft** Write a paragraph. Use new words from the unit. Use the ideas in your chart.
3. **Revise** Read your paragraph. Use the Revising Checklist to correct errors.

Revising Checklist

- ✔ Did I tell about two friends?
- ✔ Did I say how they are alike and different?

Here is Miguel's paragraph.

I have two good friends, Omar and Juan. They are the same in some ways. Omar and Juan ~~is~~ are both good at soccer. They are both seven. They both ~~has~~ have big families. They are also different. Omar likes math and science. Juan likes English.

4 **Edit** Trade papers. Correct your partner's paragraph. Use the Editing Checklist.

5 **Publish** Make a clean copy of your paragraph. Share it with the class.

Editing Checklist

- ✔ The subjects and verbs agree.
- ✔ Verb tenses are correct.
- ✔ There are different sentence lengths, patterns, and connecting words (*and*).

WB 153–154

Fluency

For Each Reading...

1. Listen to the sentences. Use your finger to follow the words.
2. Read aloud for one minute. Count the number of words you read.

Max and Ray are friends.	5
Max likes math best.	9
He is good at adding. Ray likes	16
spelling best.	18
Ray can spell and print well.	24
Max and Ray play cool music	30
together.	31
They have fun at school and fun	38
at play.	40

3. Now read for your teacher.

WB 155–156

A

about

Savanna learns **about** art.

after

He took the pumpkin home **after** he picked it.

again

They visit their family **again**.

all

We **all** worked in the garden.

animals

Animals are colorful.

another

Here comes **another** friend.

B

baby

This is a **baby**.

backpack

I wear my **backpack** to school.

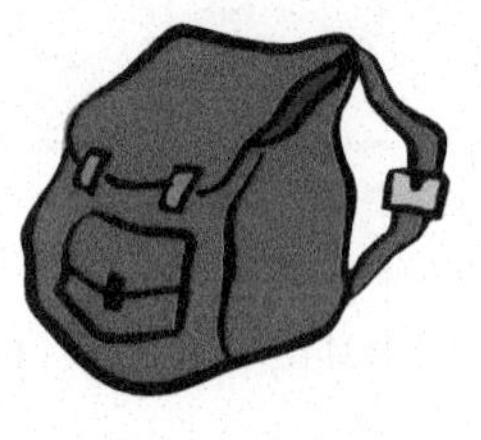

ball

I play with my **ball**.

be

Getting mail can **be** fun.

because

Ducks swim **because** they live in water.

before

Sam looked at her new school **before** she went in.

best

Gus and Shawn are **best** friends.

big

Horses are **big**.

birds

Birds eat seeds on the ground.

blossom

It is a pretty **blossom**.

blue

This mask is **blue**.

bought

He **bought** a snack.

build

The community helps **build** a house.

butterfly

A **butterfly** has pretty wings.

C

carnival

We go to the **carnival**.

celebration

A **celebration** is a special time.

cello

My cousin Sam plays the **cello** really well.

chef

My dad is a **chef**.

come

He will **come** to take her package.

community

Joe likes living in his **community**.

costume

He wears a **costume**.

country

Each **country** has its own flag.

crew

The ship has a big **crew**.

cruise

My family went on a **cruise**.

D

delicious

Carrots are a **delicious** food.

different

Owen and Mzee are **different** animals.

doctor

The **doctor** helps me get well.

dragon

This **dragon** is made of paper.

duckling

The **duckling** is small.

E

eat

Some people like to **eat** with chopsticks.

enjoy

They really **enjoy** listening to music.

envelopes

Coins are inside the red **envelopes**.

F

feathers

Birds have **feathers**.

first

First, the family eats.

food chain

Plants and animals are part of the **food chain**.

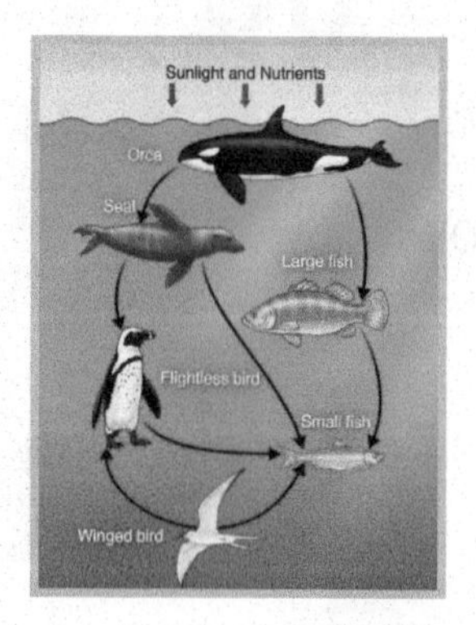

friends

These two boys are **friends**.

frog

A **frog** jumps and swims.

from

Joe takes a soccer ball **from** his bag.

fun

A party is **fun**.

G

green

These leaves are **green**.

grow

We water the plants so they will **grow**.

H

have

They **have** a ball.

he

He helps Tracey feel better.

hippopotamus

A **hippopotamus** is a big animal.

I

is

Ted **is** fat.

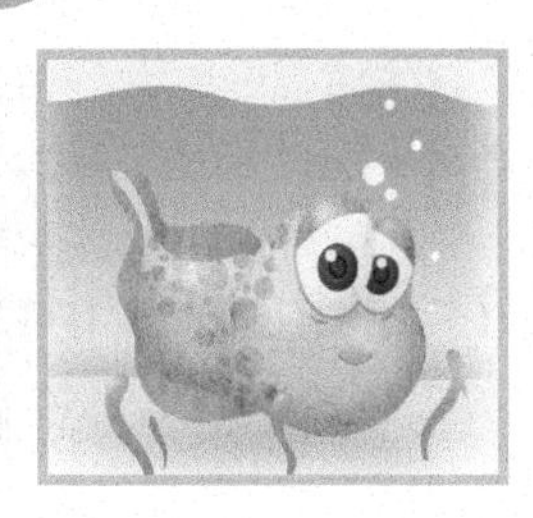

know

I **know** how to fly a kite.

A B C D E F G H I J K L M N O P Q R S T U V W X Y Z

letter

Jim writes a **letter** to send to José.

like

I **like** bedtime.

little

The kitten is **little**.

live

I **live** in a busy city.

look

I **look** far away.

M

many

There are **many** bees in the tree.

me

Kelly gave **me** a snack.

meet

We **meet** nice people in our community.

music

A horn can make **music**.

my

I wear **my** new backpack to school.

neighborhood

I live in a **neighborhood**.

new

That hat is **new**.

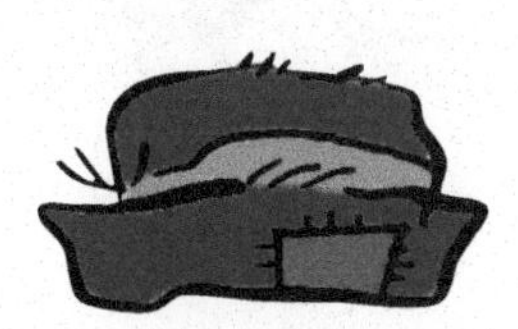

of

I have a lot **of** friends.

one

Joe has **one** soccer ball.

open

The baby's mouth is **open**.

our

We are proud of **our** flag.

out

Dahlia holds her hands **out**.

over

Can they go **over** the bar?

P

package

A **package** came today.

parade

They played in a **parade**.

people

The **people** are proud.

play

We like to **play** football.

project

We worked on a **project**.

pumpkin

The **pumpkin** is orange.

S

see

I **see** Ted. Ted sees me.

she

She is a vet.

snack

This **snack** tastes good.

so

The duck is **so** small.

soccer

I play **soccer**.

symbol

A flag is a **symbol** of a country.

the

The boy likes his drink.

then

I do my work. **Then** I go out to play.

they

They sort packages.

this

This letter is for Billy.

three

I eat **three** times a day.

to

They like **to** drum.

together

Max and Ray solve the problem **together**.

too

The hat is **too** big.

tortoise

A **tortoise** is slow.

two

There are **two** boys and **two** balls.

U

use

I can **use** a pen.

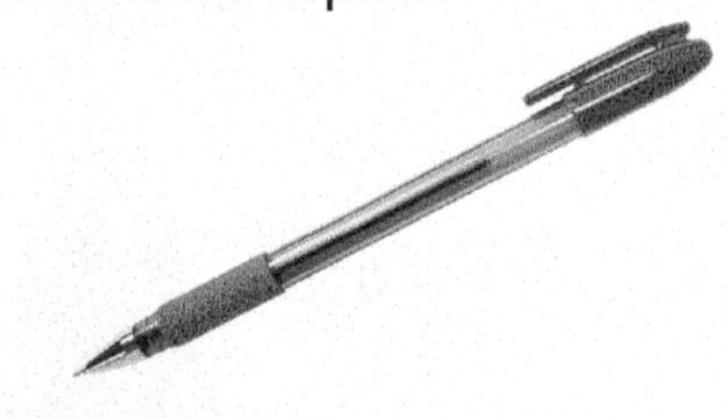

W

waddle

A duck can **waddle**.

wants

The duckling **wants** to come out of the egg.

water

Water is in a lake.

welcome

Welcome to our home!

where

Where do you live? Do you live in the United States?

white

The duck is **white**.

why

Why are the plants near the window?

with

We celebrate **with** each other.

work

The boys **work** together to fix the box.

worked

Martin **worked** hard sending packages.

Y

you

I give the book to **you**.

Index

Index

Credits

COVER: CS1_U1_SE_Cover Brian Jackson/123RF

FM ix Wavebreak Media Ltd/123RF; x Peter M. Wilson/Alamy Stock Photo; xi Artistic Photo/Shutterstock; xii Buncha Lim/Shutterstock; xv Trabantos/Shutterstock; xvi Peter Greste/Reuters.

UNIT 1 002–003 Syda Productions/Shutterstock; 004 (T) Carla Mestas/Pearson Education, Inc.; 004 (CL) Michelle Lee Photography/Shutterstock; 004 (CR) Jarenwicklund/123RF; 004 (B) Tobkatrina/Shutterstock; 005 (T) Vladitto/Shutterstock; 005 (C) Mishoo/123RF; 005 (B) Studio 8/Pearson Education Ltd; 006 (L) Yan Lev/Shutterstock; 006 (R) XiXinXing/Shutterstock; 007 Bestweb/Shutterstock; 007 (R Inset) Ndul/123RF; 008 (T) Jonathan Cohen/iStock/Getty Images; 008 (B) Espies/Shutterstock; 020 (T) 123RF; 020 (B) Andy Dean Photography/Shutterstock; 022 (T) Jiri Hera/Shutterstock; 022 (C) Steven Russell Smith Photos/Shutterstock; 022 (B) Igor Gorelchenkov/Shutterstock; 036 (T) Andersen Ross/Blend Images/Alamy Stock Photo; 036 (C) St-fotograf/Shutterstock; 036 (B) Africa Studio/Shutterstock; 037 (T) Dmitry Naumov/Shutterstock; 037 (C) Fotokostic/Shutterstock; 037 (B) Yellowj/Shutterstock; 038 (T) Jamie Grill/JGI/Blend Images/Getty Images; 038 (C) Mama Belle Love kids/Shutterstock; 038 (B) Dragon Images/Shutterstock; 048 Blend Images/123RF; 050 Wavebreakmedia/iStock/Getty Images; 050–051 Wavebreakmedia Ltd PHBTS/Alamy Stock Photo; 054 Monkey Business Images/Shutterstock; 055 Dolgachov/123RF.

UNIT 2 058–059 Yellow Dog Productions/DigitalVision/Getty Images; 060 (T) Matteo Colombo/DigitalVision/Getty Images; 060 (B) Basphoto/123RF; 061 (T) Pressmaster/Shutterstock; 061 (B) Hero Images/Getty Images; 064 (T) Pressmaster/Shutterstock; 064 (B) Andrey_Popov/Shutterstock; 076 (T) Hero Images Inc./Alamy Stock Photo; 076 (B) Denis Radovanovic/Shutterstock; 078 (T) Imagemore Co, Ltd./Getty Images; 078 (B) Patrick Foto/Shutterstock; 088 (T) Fotoluminate LLC/Shutterstock; 088 (B) Muellek Josef/Shutterstock; 089 S_oleg/Shutterstock; 090 (T) Bondarchuk/Shutterstock; 090 (C) Jackf/123RF; 090 (B) Franck Boston/123RF; 092 Wavebreak Media Ltd/123RF; 093 Wavebreak Media Ltd/123RF; 094 Wavebreak Media Ltd/123RF; 095 Wavebreak Media Ltd/123RF; 096 Wavebreak Media Ltd/123RF; 097 Nestor Rizhniak/Shutterstock; 098 Gpointstudio/iStock/Getty Images; 099 Wavebreak Media Ltd/123RF; 100 (T) Ian Allenden/123RF; 100 (C) Andriy Popov/123RF; 100 (B) Simonkr/E+/Getty Images; 101 (T) Kzenon/123RF; 101 (B) Stephen Coburn/Shutterstock; 102 (T) Cyndi Monaghan/Moment/Getty Images; 102 (B) Lara65/Shutterstock; 103 Baldur Pan Photography/Moment Open/Getty Images; 104 Yellow Dog Productions/DigitalVision/Getty Images; 104–105 Hero Images/Getty Images; 106 Photonikaagency/Shutterstock; 108 Kokhanchikov/Shutterstock; 110 (T) OZMedia/Shutterstock; 110 (B) David Lee/Shutterstock; 111 Wavebreak Media Ltd/123RF.

UNIT 3 112–113 Barna Tanko/Alamy Stock Photo; 114 (T) Filmfoto-03edit/Alamy Stock Photo; 114 (B) Jim West/Alamy Stock Photo; 115 (T) Kirin_photo/iStock/Getty Images; 115 (B) Mctaay/Shutterstock; 116 (T) Tom Merton/Caiaimage/Getty Images; 116 (B) Blend Images - Stewart Cohen/Brand X Pictures/Getty Images; 117 (L) Kzenon/Shutterstock; 117 (R) Monkey Business Images/Shutterstock; 118 (T) XiXinXing/Shutterstock; 118 (B) Fotografiche/Shutterstock; 120 (T) Discpicture/Alamy Stock Photo; 120 (CL) M_a_y_a/iStock/Getty Images; 120 (CR) Coxy58/Shutterstock; 120 (B) Fotolinchen/iStock/Getty Images; 121 Keren Su/Getty Images; 122 D. Hurst/Alamy Stock Photo; 123 Keren Su/Getty Images; 124 (Inset) Fotolinchen/iStock/Getty Images; 124–125 Guido Fuà/AGF Srl/Alamy Stock Photo; 125 (Inset) Afhunta/123RF; 126 (Inset) M_a_y_a/iStock/Getty Images; 126–127 Delpixel/Shutterstock; 128 Coxy58/Shutterstock; 129 Fotolinchen/iStock/Getty Images; 130 (T) Jose Gil/Shutterstock; 130 (B) Peter M. Wilson/Alamy Stock Photo; 131 (T) Woodys Photos/Shutterstock; 131 (B) Gwengoat/iStock/Getty Images; 134 (a) Osabee/Shutterstock; 134 (b) Kali9/E+/Getty Images; 134 (c) Puay Ng/EyeEm/Getty Images; 134 (d) Mihai Andritoiu/Alamy Stock Photo; 136 (TL) Lane Oatey/Getty Images; 136 (TR) Tanachot Srijam/Shutterstock; 136 (BL) Jakkrit Orrasri/Shutterstock; 136 (BR) Asia Images/Getty Images; 137 Osabee/Shutterstock; 138–139 Lane Oatey/Getty Images; 140 Lane Oatey/Getty Images; 141 Asia Images/Getty Images; 142 Osabee/Shutterstock; 143 Jakkrit Orrasri/Shutterstock; 144 Windmoon/Shutterstock; 145 Tanachot Srijam/Shutterstock; 146 Lane Oatey/Getty Images; 147 Jakkrit Orrasri/Shutterstock; 148 (T) Ondrej Prosicky/Shutterstock; 148 (B) Monkey Business Images/Shutterstock; 150 (T) Shnycel/Shutterstock; 150 (C) Rawpixel.com/Shutterstock; 150 (B) Yang Yu/123RF; 152 Artistic Photo/Shutterstock; 153 Artistic Photo/Shutterstock; 154 Nurlan Valiyev/Shutterstock; 155 Sergey Novikov/Shutterstock; 156 Rich Graessle/Icon Sportswire CGV/Newscom; 157 Len Holsborg/Alamy Stock Photo; 158–159 Dpa Picture Alliance/Alamy Stock Photo; 160 Artistic Photo/Shutterstock; 161 Rich Graessle/Icon Sportswire CGV/Newscom; 164 Barna Tanko/Alamy Stock Photo; 164–165 Subodhsathe/iStock/Getty Images ; 168 A3pfamily/Shutterstock; 171 (T) D. Hurst/Alamy Stock Photo; 171 (C) Jakkrit Orrasri/Shutterstock; 171 (B) Sergey Novikov/Shutterstock.

UNIT 4 002–003 Bill Brooks/Moment/Getty Images; 004 (T) Sofarina79/Shutterstock; 004 (B) Denis Dryashkin/123RF; 005 (T) Martin Mecnarowski/Shutterstock; 005 (C) Catalin Petolea/Shutterstock; 005 (B) Anna Issakova/Shutterstock; 008 (a) Blacqbook/Shutterstock; 008 (b) DMS Foto/Shutterstock; 008 (c) Evastudio/Shutterstock; 008 (d) Sean Paul William Murphy/Shutterstock; 010 (TL) Goinyk/123RF; 010 (TR) Tsekhmister/Shutterstock; 010 (B) GlobalP/iStock/Getty Images; 011 (T) Tsekhmister/Shutterstock; 011 (B) Tsekhmister/Shutterstock; 012 Ian_Sherriffs/Shutterstock; 013 Anneka/Shutterstock; 014 Tsekhmister/iStock/Getty Images; 015 Goinyk/123RF; 016 Buncha Lim/Shutterstock; 017 GlobalP/iStock/Getty Images; 018 Tsekhmister/Shutterstock; 019 Buncha Lim/Shutterstock; 022 (a) Anatolii Mikhailov/Shutterstock; 022 (b) Ofisser86/123RF; 022 (c) Koldunov/Shutterstock; 022 (d) Romiana Lee/Shutterstock; 024 (a) Tudor Photography/Pearson Education, Inc.; 024 (b) Larry Korb/Shutterstock; 024 (c) Aliaksandr Mazurkevich/123RF; 024 (d) Casther/Shutterstock; 024 (e) Nattika/Shutterstock; 024 (f) Maya Kruchankova/Shutterstock; 024 (g) Rafał Olechowski/123RF; 025 Iianem/123RF; 026 Ianlangley/123RF; 027 (T) Cloud7days/123RF; 027 (B) Nattika/Shutterstock; 028 Swapan Photography/Shutterstock; 029 Larry Korb/Shutterstock; 030 Cristi180884/Shutterstock; 031 Brandon Bourdages/Shutterstock; 032 Maya Kruchankova/Shutterstock; 033 Cristi180884/Shutterstock; 034 Casther/Shutterstock; 035 Rafał Olechowski/123RF; 036 (a) Jana Kleteckova/123RF; 036 (b) Purplequeue/123RF; 036 (c) Anton Havelaar/Shutterstock; 036 (d) Geza Farkas/Shutterstock; 036 (e) Makarova Viktoria/Shutterstock; 038 (T) Paula French/Shutterstock; 038 (BL) This World Photography/Shutterstock; 038 (BC) Charles Brutlag/Shutterstock; 038 (BR) Marcel Mooij/Shutterstock; 052 Bill Brooks/Moment/Getty Images; 052–053 Jurgens Potgieter/Shutterstock; 054 Bouvier Sandrine/123RF; 056 Age

Credits

fotostock/Alamy Stock Photo; 059 (T) GlobalP/iStock/Getty Images; 059 (B) Ianlangley/123RF.

UNIT 5 060–061 Monkey Business Images/Shutterstock; 062 (T) Jeremy Horner/Alamy Stock Photo; 062 (B) Sianc/Shutterstock; 063 (TL) Marcduf/iStock Unreleased/Getty Images; 063 (TR) Jordan Tan/Shutterstock; 063 (B) Moodboard/Alamy Stock Photo; 066 (T) Best Photo Studio/Shutterstock; 066 (C) Aman Ahmed Khan/Shutterstock; 066 (B) Digital Media Pro/Shutterstock; 080 (TL) Fever pitched/123RF; 080 (TR) Studio1one/123RF; 080 (B) Oleksiy Rezin/Shutterstock; 082 (T) Serena Hsu/Zuma Press/Newscom; 082 (C) C12/Shutterstock; 082 (B) FPG/Staff/Archive Photos/Getty Images; 084 (TL) Serena Hsu/Zuma Press/Newscom; 084 (TR) Bill Johnson/Denver Post/Contributor/Getty Images; 084 (BL) Nikonaft/Shutterstock; 084 (BR) FPG/Staff/Archive Photos/Getty Images; 085 C12/Shutterstock; 086 Serena Hsu/Zuma Press/Newscom; 087 Nikonaft/Shutterstock; 088 Bill Johnson/Denver Post/Contributor/Getty Images; 089 C12/Shutterstock; 090 Bettmann/Contributor/Getty Images; 091 FPG/Staff/Archive Photos/Getty Images; 092 Patrick van Katwijk/Dpa picture alliance/Alamy Stock Photo; 093 Serena Hsu/Zuma Press/Newscom; 096 (T) Stocky images/123RF; 096 (C) Cruise Ships/Alamy Stock Photo; 096 (B) Christian Goupi/Age Fotostock/Alamy Stock Photo; 098 (TL) Stocky images/123RF; 098 (TR) Christian Goupi/Age Fotostock/Alamy Stock Photo; 098 (B) 123RF; 099 Jochen Tack/Alamy Stock Photo; 100 Steve Debenpor/iStock/Getty Images; 101 Holger Leue/Lonely Planet Images/Getty Images; 102 Celso Diniz/Shutterstock; 103 Andresr/E+/Getty Images; 104 Dave G. Houser/Alamy Stock Photo; 105 Claudio Ventrella/iStock/Getty Images; 106 Trabantos/Shutterstock; 107 Andresr/E+/Getty Images; 108 Richard Uhlhorn/Alamy Stock Photo; 109 Stuart Forster/Alamy Stock Photo; 112 Monkey Business Images/Shutterstock; 112–113 Fat Camera/E+/Getty Images; 116 Bluefish_ds/Shutterstock.

UNIT 6 120–121 Monkey business images/iStock/Getty Images; 122 (T) Tinna2727/123RF; 122 (B) Sergey Novikov/Shutterstock; 123 (T) Darrin Henry/Shutterstock; 123 (B) Svitlana Bezuhlova/Shutterstock; 126 (T) Stockbroker/123RF; 126 (C) Iakov Filimonov/123RF; 126 (B) Naluwan/Shutterstock; 138 (TL) Yuganov Konstantin/Shutterstock; 138 (TR) Yuganov Konstantin/Shutterstock; 138 (BL) Yuganov Konstantin/Shutterstock; 138 (BR) Teri Virbickis/Shutterstock; 140 (T) Randy Duchaine/Alamy Stock Photo; 140 (C) Martin Maritz/Shutterstock; 140 (B) Katatonia82/Shutterstock; 142 (L) Alberto Loyo/Shutterstock; 142 (R) Vaclav Sebek/Shutterstock; 143 Peter Greste/Reuters; 144 (T) Tantrik71/Shutterstock; 144 (B) M Reel/Shutterstock; 145 Peter Greste/Reuters; 146 Olgysha/Shutterstock; 147 Mind Storm/Shutterstock; 148 Anna Om/Shutterstock; 149 Stanislav Beloglazov/Shutterstock; 150–151 Vaclav Sebek/Shutterstock; 152 Peter Greste/Reuters; 153 Anna Om/Shutterstock; 154 M Reel/Shutterstock; 155 Seasoning_17/Shutterstock; 156 (T) Tony Garcia/Image Source/Getty Images; 156 (B) Flashpop/DigitalVision/Getty Images; 158 (T) Belchonock/123RF; 158 (TC) Sonya Etchison/Shutterstock; 158 (BC) PjrTravel/Alamy Stock Photo; 158 (B) Lopolo/Shutterstock; 170 (T) CreativeNature.nl/Shutterstock; 170 (C) Allanw/Shutterstock; 170 (B) Rck953/123RF; 172 Monkey business images/iStock/Getty Images; 172–173 Rawpixel.com/Shutterstock; 174 Anurak Ponapatimet/123RF; 176 (L) PaylessImages/123RF; 176 (R) Ronnachai Palas/123RF.

EM 180 (a) Pressmaster/Shutterstock; 180 (b) Romiana Lee/Shutterstock; 180 (c) Iakov Filimonov/123RF; 180 (d) Hero Images/Getty Images; 180 (e) Ondrej Prosicky/Shutterstock; 180 (f) Carla Mestas/Pearson Education, Inc.; 181 (a) GlobalP/iStock/Getty Images; 181 (b) Blend Images/123RF; 181 (c) Makarova Viktoria/Shutterstock; 181 (d) Fotolinchen/iStock/Getty Images; 182 (a) Hero Images/Getty Images; 182 (b) Peter M. Wilson/Alamy Stock Photo; 182 (c) C12/Shutterstock; 182 (d) Stocky images/123RF; 182 (e) Stephen Coburn/Shutterstock; 182 (f) Rawpixel.com/Shutterstock; 182 (g) Afhunta/123RF; 183 (a) Yang Yu/123RF; 183 (b) Christian Goupi/Age Fotostock/Alamy Stock Photo; 183 (c) 123RF; 183 (d) Dmitry Naumov/Shutterstock; 183 (e) Peter Greste/Reuters; 183 (f) Jakkrit Orrasri/Shutterstock; 183 (g) Lane Oatey/Getty Images; 183 (h) Naluwan/Shutterstock; 184 (a) Osabee/Shutterstock; 184 (b) Lane Oatey/Getty Images; 184 (c) Darrin Henry/Shutterstock; 184 (d) XiXinXing/Shutterstock; 184 (e) Aliaksandr Mazurkevich/123RF; 185 (a) Koldunov/Shutterstock; 185 (b) Dragon Images/Shutterstock; 185 (c) Pressmaster/Shutterstock; 185 (d) Muellek Josef/Shutterstock; 186 (a) Jiri Hera/Shutterstock; 186 (b) Didier Zylberyng/Alamy Stock Photo; 186 (c) Blacqbook/Shutterstock; 186 (d) Jamie Grill/JGI/Blend Images/Getty Images; 187 (a) Espies/Shutterstock; 187 (b) Kali9/E+/Getty Images; 187 (c) Rich Graessle/Icon Sportswire CGV/Newscom; 188 (a) Best Photo Studio/Shutterstock; 188 (b) Tinna2727/123RF; 188 (c) Wavebreak Media Ltd/123RF; 188 (d) Hill Street Studios/Blend Images/Getty Images; 189 (a) Ian_Sherriffs/Shutterstock; 189 (b) Nurlan Valiyev/Shutterstock; 189 (c) Patrick Foto/Shutterstock; 189 (d) Tinna2727/123RF; 189 (e) Simonkr/E+/Getty Images; 190 (a) Gwengoat/iStock/Getty Images; 190 (b) Mama Belle Love kids/Shutterstock; 190 (c) Bondarchuk/Shutterstock; 190 (d) Evastudio/Shutterstock; 190 (e) Tsekhmister/iStock/Getty Images; 191 (a) Shnycel/Shutterstock; 191 (b) Buncha Lim/Shutterstock; 191 (c) Anatolii Mikhailov/Shutterstock; 191 (d) Lane Oatey Getty Images; 191 (e) Andriy Popov/123RF; 191 (f) Jonathan Cohen/iStock/Getty Images.